The
LEO
Path
YOUR DAILY 2026 HOROSCOPE GUIDE

AMANDA M CLARKE

Copyright © Amanda M Clarke 2026
KORU Publishing

All rights reserved. All content, materials, and intellectual property in this book or any other platform owned by Koru Publishing are protected by copyright laws. This includes text, images, graphics, videos, audio, software, and any other form of content that may be produced by Koru Publishing.

No part of this content may be reproduced, distributed, or transmitted in any form or by any means without the prior written permission of Koru Publishing. This means that you cannot copy, reproduce, or use any of the content in this book for commercial or personal purposes without the express written consent of Koru Publishing.

Unauthorized use of any copyrighted material owned by Koru Publishing may result in legal action being taken against you. Koru Publishing reserves the right to pursue all available legal remedies against any individual or entity found to be infringing on its copyright.

In summary, Koru Publishing © 2024 holds exclusive rights to all the content produced by it, and any unauthorized use of such content will result in legal action.

KORU Publishing

KORU (Maori;NZ)
A symbol of spiritual growth and spiritual connection.

Rocky Point Townhouse, CHRISTMAS ISLAND, Western Australia 6798

ISBN: 978-1-923614-05-5

More on the Bookshelves at www.theliteraryoracle.com

Disclaimer: The Leo Path: Your daily 2026 horoscope guide book provides information on astrological readings and intuitive interpretations, it is not intended as a substitute for professional advice, diagnosis, or treatment. The information contained in this book is provided for educational and entertainment purposes only and is not meant to be taken as specific advice for individual circumstances. The author and publisher make no representations or warranties with respect to the accuracy or completeness of the contents of this book and specifically disclaim any implied warranties of merchantability or fitness for a particular purpose. The reader should always consult with a licensed professional for any specific concerns or questions. The author and publisher shall not be liable for any loss or damage caused or alleged to have been caused, directly or indirectly, by the information contained in this book. The use of this book is at the reader's sole risk

More from Amanda Clarke
The Literary Oracle
www.theliteracyoracle.com

The "Daily Guidance" series offers an innovative approach to finding spiritual wisdom and practical advice. Each book in the series is a unique tool designed for daily introspection and decision-making. Readers are invited to meditate on a question or seek general guidance for the day, then flip to a random page in the book. The page they land on provides a personalized message from various spiritual sources, such as angels, tarot, or spirit animals. With each turn of the page, these books deliver insightful, positive messages and mantras to inspire personal growth and provide clarity on life's daily challenges and decisions.

Other books in this series:-
The Angelic Oracles
Daily Angel Tarot Reading
Mystic Tarot Cat
Oracle of the Tarot Cat
Vibes Unveiled
Spirit Animal Oracle
Answers from the Oracles
Messages from the Angels

Supporting Indie Authors

Love your daily guidance? You can grab more of my books direct from The Literary Oracle: www.theliteraryoracle.com

Buying direct means:
- Much better prices for you + free shipping.
- More support for me as an indie author
- More magical books in your hands

My books are also available worldwide through online bookstores, but direct purchases help keep the magic flowing.

Thank you for supporting indie creativity!

Scan me

Welcome to The Leo Path: Your Daily 2026 Horoscope Guide — your bold, heart-led companion for the year ahead. Crafted for the radiant, courageous, and generous Leo, this guide honors the way you move through life — with confidence, creativity, and a soul that thrives when it shines brightly.

Inside, you'll find daily horoscopes paired with affirmations designed to align with your natural strengths. Each page offers guidance to help you move through 2026 with clarity and fire — whether you're pursuing ambitious goals, deepening love and friendships, nurturing your creative spark, or leading with authenticity and pride.

This isn't about forcing outcomes — it's about aligning with your brilliance. As you turn each page, you'll receive reminders, encouragement, and cosmic insights urging you to embrace your power and trust your inner flame. Let this be the year you shine fully, love boldly, and celebrate the magic of living in harmony with your heart and the stars.

The Answers You Seek

Are Within

January 2026

Leo
01 January 2026

Leo, the year opens with a burst of solar fire for you. The Moon highlights your creative house, urging you to step into 2026 with unapologetic confidence. Don't be surprised if old doubts briefly echo today, but let them fade—your energy is far bigger than fear. You're being called to set intentions that feel bold, not safe. This is a day for writing down desires, affirming your place in the world, and choosing joy over hesitation. The spotlight naturally seeks you—embrace it.

Affirmation & Gratitude

"I welcome 2026 with boldness, gratitude, and the courage to shine brighter than ever before in my life."

Leo
02 January 2026

Today your ruling Sun works harmoniously with Mercury, sharpening your mind and your ability to speak with authority. Don't underestimate how much people listen when you talk now—your words land with weight. Whether it's a casual chat, a heartfelt conversation, or a declaration of goals, you're planting seeds that will grow. Relationships benefit from your warmth and honesty. If others hesitate, keep moving forward with your plans; your confidence will inspire them to follow later.

Affirmation & Gratitude

"My words carry strength, love, and vision. I use them to inspire myself and those around me today."

Leo
03 January 2026

The Moon's energy today pulls your attention inward, encouraging reflection and rest. Though Leos thrive in the spotlight, even you need a pause to gather strength. Don't push against the slower pace; instead, take time for journaling, meditation, or simply enjoying your own company. This isn't retreat—it's recharging. Financially, an intuitive hunch could surface, so listen closely. A trusted friend may share advice that proves valuable later. Quiet doesn't diminish your power; it prepares you for greater leaps.

Affirmation & Gratitude

"I honor my need for rest, trusting that pausing strengthens my body, mind, and spirit for what's next."

Leo
04 January 2026

Venus blesses your connections today, making this an ideal time for love, laughter, and social warmth. If you're partnered, plan something that rekindles affection. If single, be open—someone may notice your charm in unexpected ways. Professionally, this glow works for you, too, helping you attract allies or mentors who appreciate your natural charisma. Remember, Leo, when you radiate joy, the universe matches your vibration. Don't shy away from compliments; they're mirrors reminding you of your worth.

Affirmation & Gratitude

"I attract love, friendship, and opportunities by sharing my authentic self with warmth, generosity, and openness."

Leo
05 January 2026

Mars energizes your career zone, sparking motivation to tackle projects or make bold moves. This is not the time to play small—take initiative. A conversation with a superior could open unexpected doors. Though some resistance may arise, your determination overrides it. Just pace yourself so enthusiasm doesn't turn into burnout. Networking also proves powerful today; reach out to someone you've been meaning to connect with. Your leadership qualities are undeniable now—own them without apology.

Affirmation & Gratitude

"I am courageous in my work, embracing challenges as steppingstones to greater leadership and success."

Leo
06 January 2026

The Moon highlights your partnerships, reminding you to balance independence with collaboration. Today, cooperation brings better results than going solo. A partner, friend, or colleague may share an insight that shifts your perspective, helping you see a challenge differently. Don't dismiss compromise as weakness—it's wisdom. In love, listen more than you speak; this opens doors to deeper connection. Your Leo pride thrives when respected, but it grows stronger when paired with empathy and patience.

Affirmation & Gratitude

"I honor the voices of others while standing firm in my truth, knowing balance creates lasting harmony."

Leo
07 January 2026

Jupiter amplifies your adventurous spirit, pushing you to think bigger about what's possible in 2026. Travel, study, or bold new ventures are favored now. Even if circumstances don't allow immediate action, start planning. This is the day to dream beyond limits. Be mindful, though, that your fiery enthusiasm doesn't overlook practical details. Share your vision—it will ignite excitement in others. Your natural ability to lead isn't just for show; it's for building something lasting and expansive.

Affirmation & Gratitude

"I embrace big dreams with faith and courage, knowing the universe expands when I dare to believe."

Leo
08 January 2026

The cosmic energy today highlights balance between work and self-care. Your drive to achieve is high, but so is the need to nourish your body and mind. Avoid stretching yourself too thin just to please others. A small change in routine—like adjusting sleep, diet, or exercise—can bring huge rewards now. Emotionally, you might feel pulled in two directions, but remember Leo, harmony comes when you honor your limits. Your light shines brighter when you're healthy, grounded, and centered in your own rhythm.

Affirmation & Gratitude

"I care for my body, mind, and spirit, knowing balance fuels my strength and joy."

Leo
09 January 2026

The Sun aligns with Uranus, sparking sudden breakthroughs and unexpected opportunities. Today could bring a surprising conversation, a career twist, or even an inventive solution to an old issue. Stay flexible—you thrive when you adapt quickly. Though change can feel unsettling, this shift is working in your favor. Your natural charisma helps you navigate any surprise with grace. Keep an open mind and welcome the unexpected. Sometimes the universe knows exactly what you need before you do.

Affirmation & Gratitude

"I embrace unexpected change as a gift, trusting the universe to guide me toward new and exciting paths."

Leo
10 January 2026

With Mercury influencing your communication, this is a powerful day for making your case—whether in a negotiation, presentation, or heartfelt discussion. Your words hold weight and charm. Speak clearly, but also listen deeply; opportunities come when others feel heard. Writing projects also benefit now, so consider journaling or drafting plans for 2026. Leos sometimes forget the strength of their voice—it can move mountains. Use it wisely, and you'll see respect and opportunities flow toward you.

Affirmation & Gratitude

"I speak my truth with confidence and compassion, allowing my words to inspire and connect with others."

Leo
11 January 2026

The Moon pulls focus to your finances today, urging you to review budgets, spending habits, and long-term goals. Though Leos often enjoy treating themselves, today's energy supports practicality. Don't think of restraint as denial—think of it as empowerment. Small adjustments now will set the stage for prosperity later in the year. A discussion with a trusted advisor or friend could bring clarity. Remember, Leo, true abundance comes when you control money, not when money controls you.

Affirmation & Gratitude

"I manage my resources with wisdom and gratitude, knowing every choice I make strengthens my future stability."

Leo
12 January 2026

Relationships take center stage today as Venus casts a warm glow over your partnerships. You may feel more affectionate, romantic, or eager to connect with loved ones. If misunderstandings have lingered, this is the perfect time to heal them. A small gesture of kindness has the power to mend bridges. Professionally, teamwork is favored. Don't let pride prevent you from leaning on others—you'll discover cooperation enhances success. Let your heart lead, Leo; your warmth transforms connections.

Affirmation & Gratitude

"I open my heart fully, welcoming love, kindness, and cooperation into my relationships today."

Leo
13 January 2026

Energy surges as Mars drives your ambitions. You're ready to take bold steps toward goals you've been hesitant to chase. The fire in your belly won't let you sit still, Leo. Whether it's launching an idea, seeking recognition, or finally moving past a fear, the stars say: act now. Your courage inspires those around you, but remember to pace your energy—too much too soon can burn out your flame. Stay steady, focused, and fierce.

Affirmation & Gratitude

"I move with courage and determination, knowing each step I take aligns me closer to my dreams."

Leo

14 January 2026

The cosmos invites reflection today, encouraging you to pause and check your progress since the year began. Are your goals aligned with your true desires? Sometimes, Leo, your pride wants achievement for its own sake, but your soul asks for fulfillment. Don't ignore inner whispers; they guide you toward what really matters. This isn't about scrapping plans but fine-tuning them so they serve your heart. Trust yourself—you know when you're on the right path.

Affirmation & Gratitude

"I trust my inner wisdom, allowing my heart to guide my steps toward joy and purpose."

Leo
15 January 2026

Today, the Sun highlights your career zone, bringing recognition or at least acknowledgment of your recent efforts. Leos thrive on appreciation, and you may finally feel seen for the hard work you've been putting in. A superior or colleague may sing your praises. If not, don't wait—acknowledge yourself. Your growth is undeniable. This is a day to update your goals, polish your vision, and reaffirm your commitment to success. Stand tall, Leo—you've earned your place.

Affirmation & Gratitude

"I celebrate my achievements with pride, knowing recognition begins with valuing myself and my contributions."

Leo
16 January 2026

The Moon draws attention to home and family matters, asking you to balance ambition with personal roots. Perhaps a loved one needs your time, or domestic issues require focus. Don't see this as distraction—it's grounding. Your fiery energy can sometimes overlook the importance of quiet nurturing. By giving attention to your foundations, you strengthen everything else. Small acts—like sharing a meal, repairing something at home, or listening deeply—bring peace and remind you what truly matters.

Affirmation & Gratitude

"I nurture my home and loved ones, honoring the balance between ambition and the heart's roots."

Leo
17 January 2026

Venus energizes your creative and playful side, inviting joy back into your day. This isn't a time for heavy seriousness—it's for art, laughter, and self-expression. Leos shine when they remember life isn't all responsibility. Whether it's music, writing, sport, or simply joking with friends, indulge in what makes you feel alive. Romantic sparks are also possible now, so open your heart. Playfulness isn't trivial—it's essential to fueling your inner fire.

Affirmation & Gratitude

"I welcome joy, play, and creative expression, letting my spirit radiate with warmth and lightness."

Leo
18 January 2026

A wave of determination fuels you as Mars aligns with Saturn, making this an excellent day for disciplined action. Projects that require focus, persistence, or structure will thrive. Normally, your fiery spirit pushes forward with passion, but today's energy adds steady backbone. Use it wisely—map your plans, finish tasks, or build new habits. Your leadership feels grounded now, not just charismatic. People take you seriously when they see you follow through. Consistency is your superpower today.

Affirmation & Gratitude

"I blend passion with discipline, building strong foundations for lasting success and respect."

Leo
19 January 2026

Communication is highlighted as Mercury lights up your social sphere. Conversations today carry potential for new friendships, networking, or opportunities through connection. You might hear news that shifts your perspective, or someone may inspire you with a fresh idea. Don't shy away from reaching out to someone you've been meaning to call. Leo, your charm is magnetic, but your listening is just as powerful. Build bridges—you never know where they'll lead in 2026.

Affirmation & Gratitude

"I connect with openness, valuing each conversation as a doorway to wisdom and opportunity."

Leo
20 January 2026

The Sun shifts into Aquarius, your opposite sign, spotlighting partnerships. This begins a season where relationships—romantic, professional, and personal—take on more weight. You may notice dynamics shifting, with others asking more from you. Balance independence with cooperation. The lesson is clear: you shine brightest when others share in your light. Use this time to strengthen bonds, negotiate fairly, and remain open to compromise. Partnerships now can set the tone for the weeks ahead.

Affirmation & Gratitude

"I honor the balance of independence and connection, knowing strong partnerships elevate my light."

Leo
23 January 2026

The Sun and Moon align in a way that highlights personal transformation. Old habits or outdated ways of thinking are ready to be released. Leo, your light grows brighter when you shed what no longer fits. You may feel a strong urge to clean, declutter, or cut ties with draining situations. Don't fear change—it clears space for blessings. Trust that what falls away is making room for something more aligned with your spirit.

Affirmation & Gratitude

"I release what no longer serves me, creating space for growth, joy, and abundance."

Leo
24 January 2026

Energy flows strongly toward your goals today, thanks to Mars fueling motivation. You're not just dreaming—you're doing. Tasks you've postponed now feel manageable, even exciting. Channel this burst into projects that truly matter. However, be mindful not to bulldoze others with your intensity. Share your fire in ways that inspire, not overwhelm. Your natural leadership shines brightest when you uplift the team rather than trying to outshine them. Progress is yours if balanced with grace.

Affirmation & Gratitude

"I act with courage and focus, inspiring others as I move confidently toward my goals."

Leo
25 January 2026

A Full Moon rises in your sign today, Leo, and its brilliance magnifies your presence. Expect emotions to run high—yours and others'. This lunation brings clarity about who you are becoming and what needs to be left behind. You may feel an urge to step boldly into the spotlight or make a decisive change. Trust your instincts. The Full Moon is a mirror, showing you both your strengths and vulnerabilities. Embrace both with pride.

Affirmation & Gratitude

"I honor the Full Moon's light, embracing both my power and vulnerability as part of my authentic self."

Leo
26 January 2026

After yesterday's intensity, today offers grounding. The Moon shifts, encouraging rest, reflection, and gentle self-care. Don't feel guilty for slowing down—you've poured out so much energy, and replenishment is necessary. This is a good day for journaling, creative hobbies, or simply enjoying silence. Spiritually, insights may continue to surface. Capture them. Sometimes the quiet days hold the most profound revelations. Leo, your flame doesn't dim in stillness; it strengthens.

Affirmation & Gratitude

"I give myself permission to rest, knowing quiet moments fuel my strength and wisdom."

Leo

27 January 2026

Venus highlights your financial and material world, sparking opportunities for growth. This may show up as a new source of income, a gift, or clarity around spending. Pay attention to values—what you truly treasure will guide better decisions than fleeting desires. Leos sometimes splurge to feel abundant, but today the stars remind you abundance is also in gratitude. A mindful purchase or investment now sets the stage for prosperity later.

Affirmation & Gratitude

"I value abundance in all forms, making wise choices that align with gratitude and future security."

Leo
28 January 2026

Mercury stirs curiosity, bringing fresh ideas and new perspectives. Today's conversations or research could spark long-term inspiration. Be open to unusual suggestions—what seems odd at first may hold hidden brilliance. Your charisma helps attract people who can offer guidance or collaboration. Don't dismiss small chats; even casual exchanges may lead to golden opportunities. Feed your mind with learning, reading, or exploring. The universe is showing you doors—you just need to notice and knock.

Affirmation & Gratitude

"I welcome fresh ideas and conversations, trusting that knowledge and curiosity guide me toward opportunity."

Leo
29 January 2026

The Moon stirs your inner world, drawing attention to dreams, subconscious messages, and emotions you may usually keep under wraps. Leo, your pride often keeps you moving forward without pause, but today invites honesty with yourself. Journaling, meditation, or simply sitting in quiet could reveal truths that have been simmering beneath the surface. Don't dismiss them—these insights are guiding your next steps. Vulnerability isn't weakness; it's how you build authenticity in everything you do.

Affirmation & Gratitude

"I listen to the whispers of my soul, honoring vulnerability as a powerful source of strength and clarity."

Leo
30 January 2026

Today's cosmic energy favors communication and connection. Your words can open doors and repair bridges. If tension has been lingering in relationships, this is the day to extend an olive branch. Professionally, emails, meetings, or pitches go especially well—your charisma is magnetic, and people are drawn to your warmth. Be mindful, though, to let others speak, too. Balance confidence with humility and you'll find conversations today lead to opportunities that ripple into the months ahead.

Affirmation & Gratitude

"I communicate with clarity and kindness, creating harmony and opportunities through my words and listening."

Leo
31 January 2026

Energy lifts as Mars encourages ambition and action. You may feel compelled to tackle long-delayed tasks or dive into projects with fiery passion. The stars encourage movement, but caution against rushing. Channel this burst constructively: break big goals into smaller actions. Recognition is possible if you demonstrate both enthusiasm and follow-through. You're magnetic now, Leo, and others naturally look to you for leadership. Show them determination paired with grace, and doors will swing open.

Affirmation & Gratitude

"I take focused action today, channeling my passion into steps that build momentum and long-term success."

February 2026

Leo
01 February 2026

A new month begins with the Moon lighting your social zone. Friends, groups, and communities play a bigger role today. Invitations may arrive, or you may feel compelled to reach out. Networking brings benefits, but so does reconnecting with old friends. Don't underestimate your ability to inspire—your presence uplifts those around you. Share ideas openly, and you may discover someone who becomes a valuable collaborator this year. Leo, connection multiplies your brilliance.

Affirmation & Gratitude

"I open myself to community, friendships, and shared joy, knowing connection enriches my spirit and opportunities."

Leo
02 February 2026

The Sun highlights your partnership sector, putting relationships in sharp focus. Whether romantic, business, or friendship, these bonds may reveal where balance is needed. Leo, sometimes your pride wants control, but true strength comes in equality. A partner may need reassurance, or you may need to renegotiate terms. Honest conversations now strengthen ties. This is also a favorable day for contracts or agreements, as clarity is high. Approach with fairness, and harmony will follow.

Affirmation & Gratitude

"I nurture my partnerships with honesty and respect, honoring balance and equality in every relationship."

Leo
03 February 2026

The Moon energizes your career sector, bringing opportunities for progress. Recognition is likely, or at least a chance to showcase your leadership. Don't hold back —this is a day to step up, speak out, and show what you're capable of. Confidence paired with preparation ensures you shine without arrogance. Someone influential may notice your efforts, offering a path forward. Leo, your natural leadership is undeniable— today is about demonstrating substance as well as style.

Affirmation & Gratitude

"I shine in my work, letting confidence and preparation carry me toward recognition and success."

Leo
04 February 2026

Today's energy is more introspective, reminding you not to run too fast without pausing. Balance outward ambition with inner check-ins. Spiritual practices, creative hobbies, or even quiet reflection can bring clarity. You may feel pulled between responsibility and rest—choose both. Your intuition is especially sharp now; pay attention to signs and gut feelings. Though others may clamor for your attention, protect some space for yourself. Leo, when you honor your inner flame, it burns brighter.

Affirmation & Gratitude

"I balance ambition with reflection, trusting that my inner fire guides me with wisdom and strength."

Leo
05 February 2026

The Moon lights up your learning zone, sparking curiosity and a hunger for knowledge. You may feel inspired to sign up for a course, dive into a book, or explore new philosophies. Conversations with people from different backgrounds could expand your perspective. Don't ignore this urge to grow—your soul is ready for fresh insights. Travel or planning a trip is also favored today. Leo, your fire thrives when it has new fuel—feed it with wisdom.

Affirmation & Gratitude

"I embrace learning and exploration, allowing fresh knowledge to expand my vision and ignite my spirit."

Leo
06 February 2026

Relationships take the spotlight again as Venus brings warmth to your connections. Romantic energy feels especially strong—this is a day for gestures of love, affection, or even reconciliation. Professionally, partnerships also benefit; collaboration flows smoothly. If you've felt distant from someone, reach out with sincerity. Leo, your heart is generous—when you share it openly, bonds deepen. Today's stars remind you that relationships are your greatest treasures, and nurturing them multiplies your joy.

Affirmation & Gratitude

"I share love and kindness freely, knowing strong connections enrich every area of my life."

Leo
07 February 2026

Mars fuels your creativity and self-expression today. Ideas flow quickly, and you're eager to put them into action. Whether through art, writing, performance, or problem-solving, your originality shines. Don't second-guess your inspiration—trust it. Others may notice your spark and be drawn to your enthusiasm. This is also a good day for playful fun with friends or family. Leo, creativity is not indulgence; it's how your spirit roars. Let your fire be seen.

Affirmation & Gratitude

"I honor my creative fire, letting my unique spark inspire joy, originality, and expression."

Leo
08 February 2026

The Moon highlights finances again, asking you to review your resources with clarity. Expenses may surface, but so could opportunities. Avoid impulsive splurges—think long term. Consider where you can create stability rather than chasing fleeting indulgence. If you've been contemplating an investment or savings plan, today brings favorable energy to act. Abundance is not just money—it's gratitude, security, and wise stewardship. Leo, when you treat wealth as a tool, it multiplies in surprising ways.

Affirmation & Gratitude

"I manage my finances with wisdom and gratitude, trusting abundance flows when I make empowered choices."

Leo
09 February 2026

Mercury enhances communication, making this a powerful day for writing, speaking, or presenting your ideas. Conversations may carry a deeper weight, offering breakthroughs or clarity. Someone may share information that changes your perspective. Be open to learning, and don't underestimate the impact of your voice. Professionally, this is an excellent day for negotiations. Personally, honest dialogue clears the air. Leo, your words are golden when you pair confidence with sincerity. Use them wisely today.

Affirmation & Gratitude

"I use my voice with clarity and truth, inspiring others while staying true to myself."

Leo
10 February 2026

A quieter energy surrounds you, encouraging solitude and reflection. Today is less about action and more about alignment. Don't feel guilty for slowing down—it's necessary. Spiritual practices, journaling, or even long walks in nature can recharge you. Insights may come through dreams or meditation. Leo, your inner world is just as vibrant as your outer one. By reconnecting within, you find renewed strength to shine. Today, less really is more. Trust the pause.

Affirmation & Gratitude

"I embrace stillness, knowing rest restores my power and deepens my connection to truth."

Leo
11 February 2026

The Moon moves into your sign, amplifying your confidence and charisma. You'll feel energized, radiant, and ready to take center stage. Others notice your presence more than usual—expect compliments or invitations. This is an ideal day to launch something, make a bold move, or simply enjoy being seen. You don't need to force it, Leo—the world is naturally drawn to your light. Use this magnetism wisely and let it open new doors.

Affirmation & Gratitude

"I shine naturally, allowing my light to inspire and attract opportunities with ease."

Leo
12 February 2026

The Moon in your sign continues to amplify your energy, but now Saturn's influence asks for maturity and responsibility. You may feel torn between wanting to play boldly and needing to handle obligations. The key is balance—show the world that your leadership includes both charisma and reliability. Others trust you more when they see consistency. Leo, use today to demonstrate not only your sparkle but also your substance. This combination sets you apart as unforgettable.

Affirmation & Gratitude

"I balance joy with responsibility, showing the world that my light is grounded, dependable, and true."

Leo
13 February 2026

Venus sprinkles romance and harmony over your day, creating opportunities for love, affection, or simply joyful connection. If partnered, express your feelings openly. If single, keep your heart open—someone may be drawn to your warmth. Beyond romance, today favors creative expression. Music, art, or even playful conversation bring healing energy. Leo, your love is expansive; when you share it, you light up not only yourself but everyone in your orbit.

Affirmation & Gratitude

"I radiate love and joy, inviting beauty and harmony into every interaction today."

Leo

14 February 2026

Valentine's Day aligns beautifully with cosmic energy this year, enhancing passion and partnerships. Whether celebrating with a partner or honoring self-love, today is about embracing affection wholeheartedly. If emotions run high, let them—this intensity helps deepen bonds. Gifts or gestures aren't about extravagance; they're about authenticity. Leo, love is your true language, and when you speak it without pride or fear, you transform relationships. Celebrate your heart—it's your greatest power.

Affirmation & Gratitude

"I honor love in all forms, celebrating connection, authenticity, and the courage of my heart."

Leo
15 February 2026

Today shifts focus toward practicality as Mercury sharpens your problem-solving skills. This is a day for planning, organizing, and addressing details that fuel long-term success. It may feel less glamorous than the spotlight you enjoy, but it's equally powerful. Contracts, negotiations, or decision-making benefit from your clarity. Don't ignore the small print—it carries the weight of the future. Leo, discipline paired with vision turns dreams into reality. Take small but steady steps forward.

Affirmation & Gratitude

"I honor details as steppingstones, knowing discipline strengthens my vision and future success."

Leo
16 February 2026

A wave of optimism flows in as Jupiter blesses your social sphere. Friendships and group activities feel particularly rewarding. You may be invited to join something bigger than yourself, whether community-based, professional, or social. Embrace it—team energy today feeds your spirit. Your leadership in groups is natural, but remember to also listen and encourage. Leo, when you share the spotlight, everyone benefits. Collaboration now could bring opportunities that ripple far into your year.

Affirmation & Gratitude

"I welcome community and collaboration, sharing my light to uplift collective dreams."

Leo
17 February 2026

The Moon emphasizes your career once more, bringing recognition or momentum. A superior may acknowledge your efforts, or you may see progress on a project that felt stalled. This is the universe's reminder that persistence pays off. Stand tall, but don't overinflate—humility keeps your victories grounded. Celebrate your wins and keep pushing forward. Leo, you're building something lasting, and each step now is a brick in your foundation of success.

Affirmation & Gratitude

"I celebrate progress with humility, knowing persistence builds lasting success."

Leo
18 February 2026

The Sun moves into Pisces, highlighting your eighth house of transformation, intimacy, and shared resources. Expect deeper conversations and perhaps insights about trust, vulnerability, or money matters. It's not always comfortable for fiery Leo to sit with depth, but today invites healing and courage. Share openly with someone you trust, or reflect on your emotional patterns. Transformation is brewing, and it begins with honesty. The more you face, the freer you'll feel.

Affirmation & Gratitude

"I embrace transformation with courage, trusting that vulnerability brings freedom and renewal."

Leo
19 February 2026

The Moon illuminates your adventure sector, sparking curiosity and a need to explore beyond the usual. You may feel restless, craving travel, study, or something new to ignite your passion. Even if you can't leap into action today, plan ahead. Research destinations, courses, or spiritual practices that stretch your perspective. Your spirit thrives when you push beyond the ordinary. Leo, the stars remind you that growth happens outside your comfort zone—so dare to dream big today.

Affirmation & Gratitude

"I embrace new horizons, trusting each step into the unknown expands my wisdom and joy."

Leo
20 February 2026

Practical matters call for your attention today, especially around finances or shared resources. You may need to review budgets, bills, or responsibilities tied to others. Though Leo prefers the glamorous side of life, handling details now strengthens your future freedom. Approach conversations about money with openness rather than pride; cooperation ensures smoother outcomes. This is also a good day to release fear about scarcity and embrace gratitude for what you already have.

Affirmation & Gratitude

"I manage resources wisely, knowing gratitude and responsibility pave the path to abundance."

Leo
21 February 2026

Venus lights up your relationship sector, making today perfect for love and connection. If partnered, tenderness and warmth come easily. If single, your magnetic charm is hard to miss. Beyond romance, friendships or work partnerships benefit from harmony and compromise. The lesson today is balance—your natural charisma attracts, but your willingness to listen sustains. Leo, relationships are not about control but about collaboration, and the stars remind you to open your heart generously.

Affirmation & Gratitude

"I nurture love and harmony, allowing relationships to flourish with openness and trust."

Leo
22 February 2026

The Moon focuses on your inner world, stirring emotions you may usually brush aside. Pay attention to dreams, intuition, and subtle feelings—they hold guidance for you now. Instead of distracting yourself with activity, allow space for reflection. This may feel uncomfortable at first, but breakthroughs come from honesty with yourself. Spiritual practices or creative outlets can help channel this energy productively. Leo, your courage is strongest when you face your own truths.

Affirmation & Gratitude

"I honor my emotions and intuition, trusting my inner wisdom to guide me."

Leo
23 February 2026

Mars energizes your routines today, pushing you to reorganize daily habits. Whether diet, exercise, or work schedules, momentum builds when you act now. Your fiery energy thrives on structure if you choose to see it as empowerment rather than restriction. Productivity is high—tackle what you've been putting off. Don't try to do it all at once; sustainable change comes from steady effort. Leo, when you channel fire into discipline, magic happens.

Affirmation & Gratitude

"I strengthen my daily habits, knowing discipline fuels my passion and success."

Leo
24 February 2026

Mercury highlights communication in close relationships, encouraging honest dialogue. If something has been left unsaid, this is the day to voice it gently. You'll find words flow more easily, helping clear misunderstandings or spark deeper intimacy. Professionally, your ability to negotiate and mediate shines. Don't fear vulnerability—it fosters stronger bonds. Leo, your warmth paired with clear communication makes you irresistible and trustworthy today. Speak, but also listen deeply. Balance is key.

Affirmation & Gratitude

"I communicate with openness and care, building bridges of trust and understanding."

Leo
25 February 2026

A Full Moon in Virgo emphasizes your financial and self-worth zone. Something around money, values, or self-confidence reaches a turning point. You may realize a habit needs adjusting or that it's time to demand fair recognition for your efforts. This lunation encourages you to see abundance not only in material gain but in your own worth. Leo, the more you honor yourself, the more the world mirrors it back. Stand proudly in your value.

Affirmation & Gratitude

"I honor my worth, knowing abundance flows when I value myself fully."

Leo
26 February 2026

Today's energy pushes you to slow down after the intensity of yesterday's Full Moon. Give yourself space to process insights about money, self-worth, and values. Instead of rushing into action, take time to reflect on what feels sustainable. Leos sometimes leap boldly, but today's lesson is about measured steps. You may also crave solitude, so don't feel guilty if you withdraw slightly. This pause helps ground the transformations already unfolding within you.

Affirmation & Gratitude

"I honor stillness, knowing rest and reflection strengthen the foundation for future growth."

Leo
27 February 2026

Venus aligns with Jupiter, bringing a wave of optimism and charm into your relationships. Social invitations or romantic sparks could appear, and your warmth draws others effortlessly. Professionally, networking proves fruitful, and a conversation may open an unexpected door. Enjoy this lighthearted energy but also notice the opportunities it brings. Leo, when you shine authentically, you attract not only admiration but blessings. Today, your generosity of spirit is your magnet.

Affirmation & Gratitude

"I radiate warmth and joy, attracting opportunities and love with ease."

Leo
28 February 2026

The Moon activates your communication zone, making today perfect for conversations, learning, and sharing ideas. Your words carry extra power, so use them thoughtfully. Writing, teaching, or even casual chats may spark important realizations. Avoid gossip or exaggeration, as they could backfire. Instead, lean into truth and clarity. Your natural storytelling ability shines, Leo, so don't be surprised if others are drawn to your wisdom. Speak from the heart and inspire.

Affirmation & Gratitude
"I use my voice with clarity and sincerity, allowing my words to uplift and connect."

March 2026

Leo
01 March 2026

A new month begins with fresh momentum. Mars energizes your career and ambition, urging bold moves toward goals. You may feel restless if progress is slow, but patience paired with action ensures success. This is a day to pitch ideas, chase opportunities, or take steps that show commitment. Recognition may come, but the real reward is momentum. Leo, your leadership energy is magnetic—use it to carve paths others will want to follow.

Affirmation & Gratitude

"I pursue my goals with courage and consistency, trusting momentum will carry me toward success."

Leo
02 March 2026

The Sun in Pisces shines on intimacy, shared resources, and transformation. Conversations about trust, vulnerability, or finances may arise. Though these topics can feel heavy, facing them honestly deepens bonds and strengthens your future security. Don't shy away—embrace the discomfort. Healing is possible when truth replaces avoidance. Leo, remember your strength lies not just in your roar but in your courage to reveal your softer side. Authenticity today brings renewal.

Affirmation & Gratitude

"I embrace vulnerability with courage, knowing honesty opens the path to deeper trust and transformation."

Leo
03 March 2026

The Moon in your home zone draws attention to family or domestic matters. You may feel a strong urge to nest, reorganize, or simply enjoy comfort with loved ones. Work may call, but today's cosmic nudge reminds you that your foundation sustains everything else. Small acts like cooking, cleaning, or repairing create peace. Emotional conversations with family may also bring healing. Leo, when your roots are strong, your branches can stretch even higher.

Affirmation & Gratitude

"I nurture my home and family, knowing strong roots support my brightest growth."

Leo
04 March 2026

Mercury heightens curiosity and insight, making today ideal for brainstorming or research. You may stumble on an idea that excites you for the long term. Keep an open mind, because inspiration comes from unexpected places. Conversations flow easily, and someone's perspective may spark a breakthrough. Professionally, proposals and planning thrive. Personally, journaling or vision-boarding helps clarify dreams. Leo, your brilliance is magnified when you stay curious and flexible—don't cling to the familiar.

Affirmation & Gratitude

"I welcome fresh ideas with curiosity, knowing inspiration guides me toward new opportunities."

Leo
05 March 2026

Today the Moon lights up your creative and playful sector, urging you to enjoy life beyond responsibilities. Pursue hobbies, laughter, or time with children—anything that sparks joy. This energy also boosts romance, making it an ideal day to express affection or plan something fun with a partner. Professionally, creative thinking solves problems now. Don't overthink—go with what excites you. Leo, your spark inspires others when you show that fun and ambition can beautifully coexist.

Affirmation & Gratitude

"I embrace joy and creativity, letting playfulness fuel my heart and inspire those around me."

Leo
06 March 2026

Practical matters return as the Moon highlights health, routines, and organization. If you've been neglecting exercise, rest, or nutrition, today is a cosmic reminder. Productivity is strong, but only when you care for yourself first. Set realistic goals and tackle them step by step. Remember, Leo, self-discipline isn't restriction—it's empowerment. By tending to your body and daily habits, you create a strong base for your fiery ambitions to thrive long term.

Affirmation & Gratitude

"I honor my body and routines, knowing discipline supports strength, vitality, and success."

Leo
07 March 2026

Venus enhances partnerships, reminding you that love and cooperation create balance. Relationships may feel smoother, with opportunities to share affection or resolve tensions. This energy also supports professional teamwork, helping you achieve more through collaboration. If single, connections could spark through social circles or unexpected introductions. Leo, your charisma is magnetic, but relationships deepen when paired with empathy. Today is about valuing connection not as a stage but as shared warmth.

Affirmation & Gratitude

"I value love and cooperation, knowing relationships thrive through empathy and mutual respect."

Leo
08 March 2026

Mars charges your creative spirit, urging bold self-expression. You may feel restless if stuck in routine, so break free with art, music, sport, or playful activities. Professionally, innovative approaches impress others—don't be afraid to pitch unique ideas. Passion and courage define your actions today. Leos shine when authentic, and this cosmic push reminds you that originality is your gift. Stand tall and let your talents roar without hesitation.

Affirmation & Gratitude
"I express myself boldly, letting passion and creativity fuel my confidence and success."

Leo
09 March 2026

The Moon highlights your deeper emotions and subconscious, making today perfect for reflection and healing. Old fears or insecurities may resurface, not to hold you back but to be released. Journaling, meditation, or confiding in someone you trust can help process these feelings. Don't suppress them, Leo—acknowledging vulnerability strengthens you. Insights gained today will free you for bigger leaps later this month. Healing isn't weakness; it's the foundation of true power.

Affirmation & Gratitude

"I honor my emotions, releasing fears and embracing healing as a source of strength."

Leo
10 March 2026

Communication flows easily as Mercury sharpens your words and ideas. This is an excellent day for negotiations, pitches, or heartfelt discussions. You may also feel drawn to learning or sharing knowledge with others. Information surfaces that could guide future plans. Professionally, emails or meetings bring breakthroughs. Personally, conversations heal or inspire. Leo, your words carry power—use them to connect and uplift. Speak with clarity and listen with presence, and doors open.

Affirmation & Gratitude
"I communicate with clarity and purpose, allowing my words to inspire and connect."

Leo
11 March 2026

The Moon energizes your career zone, spotlighting recognition and responsibility. You may be called to lead, present, or showcase your talents. This is a chance to prove not just your charisma but your reliability. Efforts made today could leave a lasting impression on influential figures. Don't doubt yourself—step into the spotlight with confidence. Leo, your natural leadership is undeniable; when combined with preparation, success is inevitable. Let today mark another victory.

Affirmation & Gratitude

"I lead with confidence and responsibility, knowing my light inspires recognition and respect."

Leo
12 March 2026

Today's energy shifts toward community and friendships as the Moon highlights your social sector. You may feel drawn to connect with groups, whether professional networks, clubs, or simply spending time with friends. Collaborations spark new opportunities now, and your natural charisma makes you a magnetic presence in any setting. Don't hesitate to share your vision—others will rally behind you. Leo, when you combine individuality with community, your influence multiplies. Today reminds you that connection fuels growth.

Affirmation & Gratitude

"I cherish my community, sharing my light and welcoming collaboration that uplifts us all."

Leo
13 March 2026

Venus adds sparkle to your career zone, making this a favorable day for recognition or opportunities. Compliments, praise, or even an offer could surface, reminding you that others see your value. Your creative approach to work is noticed, so lean into originality. However, don't let pride turn into arrogance—grace keeps your victories long-lasting. Use this momentum to set new professional goals. Leo, your leadership glows when paired with humility and vision.

Affirmation & Gratitude

"I welcome recognition with gratitude, using success to inspire and uplift others."

Leo
14 March 2026

The Moon draws attention inward, urging rest and reflection. You may feel drained from recent social and career demands, so don't push too hard. Instead, recharge your batteries with solitude, meditation, or creative hobbies. Insights from your dreams or intuition could guide you now. This pause isn't wasted—it prepares you for the new cycle ahead. Leo, strength doesn't always roar loudly; sometimes it whispers quietly in the stillness you create for yourself.

Affirmation & Gratitude

"I honor rest and reflection, knowing quiet moments restore my inner fire."

Leo
15 March 2026

Energy lifts as the Moon moves into your sign, amplifying confidence, charisma, and magnetism. You'll feel ready to step into the spotlight again, and opportunities to showcase yourself may appear. This is an excellent day to pitch ideas, meet new people, or pursue goals requiring boldness. Others notice your presence more easily, so use this visibility to your advantage. Leo, when you walk with confidence, the world naturally follows your lead.

Affirmation & Gratitude

"I shine with natural confidence, embracing opportunities that align with my true self."

Leo
16 March 2026

With Mars fueling ambition, you may feel unstoppable today. Tasks that once felt overwhelming now seem manageable. Use this burst of energy to advance projects or tackle challenges head-on. Just be mindful not to steamroll others with your intensity—balance fire with consideration. Professionally, your drive stands out, possibly earning admiration from superiors or colleagues. Leo, your determination is a gift, but it's your ability to channel it wisely that guarantees success.

Affirmation & Gratitude

"I harness my energy with focus and purpose, turning passion into progress."

Leo
17 March 2026

Mercury brings clarity to communication, making this a great day for important conversations, negotiations, or sharing ideas. You may be asked to mediate, teach, or present. Your words inspire trust and enthusiasm now. Personally, a heartfelt chat with a loved one clears lingering misunderstandings. Leo, your ability to combine charisma with sincerity makes you unforgettable—today, use that gift to build stronger bridges and open new doors. Speak from the heart, and others listen.

Affirmation & Gratitude
"I share my truth with clarity and compassion, building bridges of trust."

Leo
18 March 2026

A spiritual or intuitive nudge may arrive today as the Moon emphasizes hidden truths and inner wisdom. Pay attention to subtle signs—dreams, synchronicities, or gut feelings carry messages. You may uncover insights about a relationship, a financial matter, or your deeper desires. Don't dismiss them; your intuition is strong now. Taking time for meditation or journaling helps ground these revelations. Leo, remember your roar is powerful, but so is your quiet knowing.

Affirmation & Gratitude

"I trust my intuition, allowing inner wisdom to guide me toward clarity and peace."

Leo
19 March 2026

The Moon highlights your partnership sector, putting focus on love, cooperation, and compromise. Relationships may demand more attention now, whether romantic, business, or friendship. A partner's needs could challenge your pride, but listening deeply creates harmony. Professionally, teamwork flourishes when you honor others' contributions. Leo, your natural leadership shines brightest when paired with humility. Today is about strengthening bonds, not dominating them. Your generosity is your gift—share it to bring balance and joy.

Affirmation & Gratitude

"I honor partnerships with openness and respect, knowing shared strength creates lasting harmony."

Leo
20 March 2026

The Sun enters Aries, igniting your ninth house of exploration, wisdom, and expansion. Energy surges for adventure, higher learning, and bold dreaming. This marks a fresh chapter where you crave growth beyond familiar boundaries. You may feel pulled toward travel, study, or spiritual exploration. Don't resist—it's your soul demanding expansion. Leo, when you stretch your horizons, your fire burns even brighter. Start planning bold moves that carry you toward bigger dreams this year.

Affirmation & Gratitude

"I embrace new horizons with courage, trusting growth awaits beyond my comfort zone."

Leo
21 March 2026

A burst of optimism surrounds you as Jupiter enhances your social connections. Friends, groups, or communities bring inspiration and opportunities. Invitations or collaborations may arrive, and your presence is warmly received. This is a reminder that your fire grows when shared with others. Don't isolate—your light is meant to illuminate. Leo, you may be asked to lead or inspire today. Step forward with grace, and others will rally to your vision.

Affirmation & Gratitude

"I shine in community, uplifting others while allowing their energy to inspire me."

Leo
22 March 2026

Today's Moon stirs your career sector, urging ambition and progress. You may feel driven to push projects forward or claim recognition. Superiors or mentors may notice your efforts, so put your best foot forward. Avoid impatience—rushing could undercut your progress. Instead, let your confidence and preparation speak. Leo, your natural ability to inspire others makes today ideal for leadership roles. Show not only passion but also reliability, and success follows.

Affirmation & Gratitude

"I step into leadership with confidence and responsibility, knowing my work speaks for itself."

Leo
23 March 2026

The cosmos shifts toward reflection today as the Moon illuminates your inner world. You may crave solitude, meditation, or simply space from demands. Pay attention to dreams and intuition—they reveal truths logic may miss. This is a day for emotional healing rather than outward achievement. Leo, vulnerability is not weakness—it's the key to balance. Allow yourself to release old patterns or fears. Stillness today seeds strength for the bold moves ahead.

Affirmation & Gratitude

"I embrace stillness, trusting my inner wisdom to guide me toward healing and strength."

Leo
24 March 2026

Energy rises again as Mars fires up your social and networking sphere. Conversations, collaborations, and group projects gain momentum. Your leadership is magnetic, drawing others to your cause. However, avoid dominating—encourage others to contribute. Together, bigger goals are possible. You may also feel compelled to advocate for a belief or cause. Leo, when you use your fire to inspire collective growth, your influence stretches far beyond the personal.

Affirmation & Gratitude

"I use my fire to inspire community, encouraging collaboration and shared success."

Leo
25 March 2026

A Lunar Eclipse in Libra magnifies your communication zone, marking turning points in how you connect with others. Conversations may reveal truths that shift relationships, or you may decide to change how you use your voice. Writing, speaking, or sharing ideas now has long-term impact. Release outdated communication patterns and embrace clarity. Leo, your roar is powerful—but today is about precision and balance. Speak from the heart, and transformation follows.

Affirmation & Gratitude

"I embrace clarity in communication, releasing the old to make way for powerful new expression."

Leo
26 March 2026

After yesterday's eclipse, the cosmic energy is softer, inviting integration. You may feel emotionally sensitive, so give yourself space to process recent insights. Communication breakthroughs may have shifted how you view relationships or your role in groups. Don't rush to act—today is about absorbing lessons. Journaling or quiet reflection helps anchor clarity. Leo, eclipses often mark endings and beginnings; this pause lets you recalibrate before stepping boldly into the next phase.

Affirmation & Gratitude

"I honor transitions with patience, allowing space for lessons to settle and guide my next steps."

Leo
27 March 2026

The Moon activates your finance sector, urging focus on money, resources, and values. You may feel the need to reassess spending or explore new income opportunities. Avoid impulsive purchases; instead, consider long-term security. A conversation about shared resources may also arise. Though money isn't always your favorite topic, Leo, handling it wisely empowers your freedom. Abundance begins with valuing yourself and directing resources toward what truly matters. Take one practical step forward today.

Affirmation & Gratitude

"I value my resources and make choices that support lasting abundance and freedom."

Leo
28 March 2026

Venus inspires creativity, romance, and joy today. You're in the mood for beauty—whether through art, music, or simply enjoying life. Relationships sparkle with extra charm, making this a perfect day for love or playful fun. Your charisma is magnetic, attracting positive attention wherever you go. Professionally, creative projects thrive under this influence. Leo, your heart is your greatest asset; when you lead with joy, everything else falls into place. Shine unapologetically.

Affirmation & Gratitude

"I radiate joy and creativity, allowing love and beauty to flow through me."

Leo
29 March 2026

The Moon highlights communication, urging you to speak your truth clearly. Conversations may carry extra weight today, especially with siblings, colleagues, or close friends. Listen as much as you talk—balance ensures understanding. Writing, studying, or sharing ideas brings breakthroughs. If something has been on your mind, now is the time to articulate it. Leo, your words inspire, but they must be rooted in sincerity. Today, honesty and kindness together open important doors.

Affirmation & Gratitude

"I speak with clarity and kindness, knowing my words can heal and inspire."

Leo
30 March 2026

The cosmos emphasizes home and family, drawing your attention to your personal foundation. Domestic responsibilities may need your care, or a family member could seek your support. Though career and ambition often dominate, today reminds you that roots sustain wings. Nurturing your home environment restores balance and gives you strength for the outside world. Leo, showing love through presence and action deepens bonds more than grand gestures. Focus on comfort, connection, and stability.

Affirmation & Gratitude
"I nurture my home and loved ones, knowing strong roots support my brightest growth."

Leo
31 March 2026

The Moon lights your self-expression sector, sparking creativity and confidence. Opportunities to showcase talents or enjoy leisure activities arrive easily. Romantic encounters may feel playful and fun, while creative projects flourish with inspiration. Children or young people may bring joy today. Professionally, think outside the box—your originality is your strength. Leo, when you embrace fun and authenticity, you naturally attract admiration. Let today remind you that joy is fuel for success.

Affirmation & Gratitude

"I embrace joy and authenticity, letting my creativity shine freely."

April
2026

Leo
01 April 2026

A new month begins with Mars energizing your routines and health sector. Motivation rises to tackle daily tasks, organize life, and strengthen physical well-being. Though it may feel mundane, this energy is powerful—it helps you build consistency. Set new intentions for routines that support your vitality. Productivity is high, so channel this momentum wisely. Leo, your roar grows louder when backed by resilience and stamina. Today's small changes create tomorrow's triumphs.

Affirmation & Gratitude
"I commit to healthy routines, knowing consistency fuels my strength and success."

Leo
02 April 2026

Today the Moon lights up your relationship sector, bringing focus to partnerships, both personal and professional. You may feel called to give more attention to a partner's needs, or to renegotiate terms in a business connection. Cooperation is key—your pride may want control, but real strength lies in balance. Be mindful not to dominate conversations. When you listen as well as lead, Leo, bonds deepen and respect grows. Harmony now lays foundations for future success.

Affirmation & Gratitude
"I honor balance in relationships, choosing cooperation and respect over control."

Leo
03 April 2026

The Sun energizes your zone of exploration, making this a perfect day for adventure, study, or broadening your horizons. You may feel inspired to research, plan a trip, or pursue higher learning. Spiritual curiosity is also strong now, and you may find insights through meditation or philosophy. Leo, your spirit thrives when challenged to grow beyond the ordinary. Feed your fire with new knowledge or experiences—today's sparks may ignite life-changing dreams.

Affirmation & Gratitude

"I embrace growth and exploration, trusting that new horizons fuel my spirit."

Leo
04 April 2026

The Moon highlights your career zone, pushing you into the spotlight. Recognition is possible today, or you may feel compelled to prove yourself through hard work. Avoid arrogance—humility enhances respect. This is an ideal time to showcase leadership or commit to ambitious plans. A superior may notice your reliability, or colleagues may admire your drive. Leo, when you blend confidence with responsibility, you set yourself apart as a true leader.

Affirmation & Gratitude
"I shine in my career with confidence and humility, inspiring respect through action."

Leo
05 April 2026

Today invites introspection as the Moon highlights your inner world. You may crave solitude or spiritual practices to recharge. Listen to dreams or subtle signs—your intuition is active and may offer guidance about relationships or goals. This quiet energy balances your fiery nature, reminding you that even lions need rest. Leo, trust that retreat isn't weakness; it's renewal. By honoring your inner world, you strengthen your ability to shine outwardly tomorrow.

Affirmation & Gratitude

"I honor rest and reflection, trusting my inner wisdom to guide me."

Leo
06 April 2026

Energy rises again as the Moon moves into your sign, amplifying charisma and vitality. You may feel ready to take bold action, whether in personal goals or public roles. Others notice you more easily now, so it's a good day to network, pitch, or showcase talents. Confidence comes naturally, but avoid steamrolling others—your light shines brightest when it uplifts, not overshadows. Leo, step into the spotlight with grace—you were made for this.

Affirmation & Gratitude
"I shine with confidence and grace, letting my light uplift those around me."

Leo
07 April 2026

Mars brings determination to your financial zone, urging you to take action on money matters. Whether tackling debt, negotiating salary, or exploring investments, today supports courage in handling resources. Be cautious of overspending—channel fiery energy into building stability instead. You may also realize it's time to value yourself more in professional settings. Leo, when you demand fair recognition, others follow. Stand tall in your worth, and abundance flows more easily.

Affirmation & Gratitude

"I take bold, wise steps toward financial security, honoring my worth and future abundance."

Leo
08 April 2026

A New Moon Solar Eclipse in Aries energizes your ninth house of exploration, bringing major shifts in learning, travel, or beliefs. This is a cosmic reset urging you to think bigger and step beyond familiar limits. Eclipses bring powerful beginnings—something may suddenly align, pushing you toward growth. Trust the unknown. Leo, your fire thrives on adventure, and this eclipse lights the path. Dare to chase dreams that once felt too bold.

Affirmation & Gratitude

"I embrace new beginnings with courage, trusting the universe to guide me into growth and expansion."

Leo
09 April 2026

The energy after yesterday's eclipse is still potent, and you may feel slightly unsettled. Big changes or realizations are integrating, so don't pressure yourself to have all the answers yet. Reflection is your friend today —review your dreams, goals, or travel plans. Conversations with mentors or wise friends could spark clarity. Leo, trust the process; sometimes the universe shifts the ground beneath you to move you toward a better path. Rest in faith.

Affirmation & Gratitude

"I trust the unfolding of change, knowing each step guides me closer to purpose."

Leo
10 April 2026

The Moon activates your career zone, highlighting ambition, recognition, and responsibility. A project may demand your attention, or you might receive acknowledgment for recent efforts. Don't shy away from leadership opportunities—this is a day to stand tall. Be cautious of pride overshadowing humility; balance is key. Leo, when you combine brilliance with reliability, others see you as both inspiring and trustworthy. Let your actions prove that your roar carries substance.

Affirmation & Gratitude
"I step into leadership with confidence, blending ambition with humility."

Leo
11 April 2026

Today's Moon pulls you inward, making solitude or self-reflection appealing. You may need time away from the noise of obligations to recharge emotionally. Pay attention to dreams, instincts, or sudden feelings—they hold valuable insights. Spiritual practices, journaling, or meditation will be especially powerful. Leo, remember your strength isn't only about external shine but also about nurturing your inner fire. The quiet truths you discover today will fuel tomorrow's bold steps.

Affirmation & Gratitude

"I listen to my inner world, trusting its wisdom to guide me forward."

Leo
12 April 2026

Energy lifts as the Moon moves into your sign, amplifying charisma, courage, and vitality. You'll feel eager to act, whether on personal projects or social opportunities. This is the time to be bold—others are drawn to your radiance. Romantic or creative sparks may also ignite. Don't hesitate to showcase your talents; recognition flows naturally when you're authentic. Leo, today's stars remind you that your natural glow is your gift—share it proudly.

Affirmation & Gratitude
"I shine brightly and authentically, attracting opportunities with ease."

Leo
13 April 2026

Mars fuels determination in your financial sector, urging decisive action. You may feel driven to budget, negotiate, or make investments. While confidence helps, avoid impulsive moves—balance fire with strategy. This is also a day to reassess self-worth. If you've been undervaluing yourself, step up. Leo, demanding fair recognition is not arrogance—it's wisdom. When you treat yourself with respect, the world reflects it back. Claim your value with courage today.

Affirmation & Gratitude

"I value myself fully, making bold and wise choices about money and worth."

Leo
14 April 2026

Mercury enhances your communication zone, making this a perfect day for writing, speaking, or teaching. Words flow with ease, and your storytelling captures attention. Professional discussions, negotiations, or presentations benefit now. Personally, a heart-to-heart clears misunderstandings. Don't hold back your truth, but remember kindness amplifies your impact. Leo, your roar inspires when paired with warmth. Share your vision confidently—today, your words are powerful tools for progress.

Affirmation & Gratitude

"I use my words with clarity and kindness, inspiring others with my truth."

Leo
15 April 2026

The Moon illuminates your home and family zone, reminding you to tend to roots and foundations. Domestic matters may need attention, or you may feel called to nurture loved ones. Simple gestures—cooking, listening, or creating comfort—bring peace. Balance ambition with home life; both are vital. Leo, when your foundation is strong, you soar higher. Today, reconnect with what grounds you—it strengthens everything else you aim for.

Affirmation & Gratitude
"I nurture my home and family, honoring the roots that support my growth."

Leo
16 April 2026

The Moon sparks creativity, self-expression, and romance today. You'll feel playful and inspired, ready to enjoy art, hobbies, or lighthearted connections. Your charm attracts attention easily, making this a great day for love or showcasing talents. Professionally, creative thinking opens new doors. Remember, Leo, joy is a magnet—it draws opportunities naturally. Don't downplay your sparkle; the world benefits when you share it unapologetically. Let laughter and inspiration fuel your momentum.

Affirmation & Gratitude

"I embrace joy and creativity, letting my light shine through playful expression."

Leo
17 April 2026

Today the Moon highlights routines, health, and organization. It's a great time to refine daily habits or reset goals for wellness. Energy is best spent on practical matters—exercise, meal planning, or clearing clutter. While it may not feel glamorous, these small steps empower your fiery ambitions. Leo, when your body and environment are in harmony, your spirit soars higher. Think of discipline not as restriction but as a foundation for freedom.

Affirmation & Gratitude

"I honor healthy routines, knowing discipline strengthens my vitality and freedom."

Leo
18 April 2026

Relationships take center stage as Venus emphasizes love and cooperation. You may feel more affectionate, or a partner could seek deeper connection. Singles may find sparks in social settings. Professionally, teamwork thrives under this influence, making collaboration smooth and rewarding. Leo, your heart is your greatest gift—when you share it openly, relationships flourish. Today is about balancing pride with tenderness; vulnerability strengthens bonds far more than dominance ever could.

Affirmation & Gratitude

"I open my heart to love and cooperation, allowing relationships to deepen."

Leo
19 April 2026

The Sun shifts into Taurus, spotlighting your career and ambitions for the next month. This is a powerful cycle for recognition, achievements, and building lasting success. You may feel a strong push to prove yourself or secure your place. Avoid impatience—steady progress beats rushed leaps. Leo, your natural charisma opens doors, but consistent effort cements your legacy. Today marks the start of a chapter where your work truly shines.

Affirmation & Gratitude

"I step confidently into my ambitions, knowing consistent effort brings recognition and success."

Leo
20 April 2026

The Moon highlights transformation, intimacy, and shared resources. Emotional depth may surface in relationships, urging honesty and vulnerability. Conversations about money, trust, or personal truths could feel intense but are necessary for growth. Instead of avoiding discomfort, lean into it—you'll emerge stronger. This is also a good day for releasing old patterns and embracing renewal. Leo, your courage to face shadows makes your light even more powerful.

Affirmation & Gratitude

"I embrace transformation with courage, knowing honesty leads to deeper trust and renewal."

Leo
21 April 2026

Energy shifts toward adventure as the Moon encourages exploration and learning. You may feel drawn to study, travel, or spiritual practices. Even small steps—like reading a new book or exploring fresh ideas—bring excitement. Don't dismiss curiosity; it's fuel for your growth. Leo, when you seek knowledge, your fire expands. Today, allow yourself to dream bigger than usual—life is offering you new horizons to claim.

Affirmation & Gratitude

"I welcome exploration and knowledge, trusting new horizons expand my spirit."

Leo
22 April 2026

The Moon energizes your career sector, bringing visibility and recognition. A project may take off, or you could be called to lead. Others notice your reliability and charisma today—don't hold back. While your pride may crave applause, focus on contribution. Success flows when passion meets responsibility. Leo, this is your reminder that you were born to shine not only for yourself but also for the greater good.

Affirmation & Gratitude

"I lead with passion and responsibility, inspiring others through my example."

Leo
23 April 2026

The Moon highlights friendships and community, encouraging you to connect with others. Group activities or social networks bring inspiration and opportunity. You may be asked to lead or contribute to a shared vision. Collaboration strengthens your influence now. Don't underestimate the power of community—it multiplies your light. Leo, your natural charisma makes you the heart of any group, but today is about lifting others as you rise.

Affirmation & Gratitude

"I celebrate community and connection, knowing together we create greater possibilities."

Leo
24 April 2026

The Moon draws attention to rest and reflection. You may feel drained from recent social demands, so take time to recharge. Intuition is heightened; pay attention to dreams or sudden insights. Today favors meditation, journaling, or simply enjoying solitude. Leo, your pride may resist stepping back, but stillness is not weakness—it's preparation. Allow space for your inner wisdom to surface; it holds the keys to your next bold move.

Affirmation & Gratitude
"I honor rest and reflection, trusting stillness strengthens my spirit."

Leo
25 April 2026

Energy lifts as the Moon moves into your sign, amplifying charisma and vitality. You'll feel eager to step into the spotlight, whether in love, work, or social situations. Others notice you more easily now, so use this energy for bold action. Pursue goals, showcase talents, or enjoy admiration. Leo, remember your light is magnetic, but true leadership shines when it uplifts others too. Share your fire with generosity.

Affirmation & Gratitude

"I shine with confidence and generosity, inspiring those around me."

Leo
26 April 2026

Venus enhances your financial sector, offering opportunities for abundance or practical improvements. You may receive good news about money, or feel inspired to manage resources better. While indulgence may tempt you, choose mindful investments. Value yourself enough to make wise decisions. Leo, financial empowerment supports your freedom to pursue passions. Today's actions plant seeds for long-term security—act with confidence but also wisdom.

Affirmation & Gratitude

"I value myself and my resources, making choices that create lasting abundance."

Leo
27 April 2026

Mercury sparks communication, making today perfect for conversations, teaching, or sharing ideas. Your words carry weight and charisma, drawing others to listen. Professionally, this is an excellent day for proposals or negotiations. Personally, heartfelt talks bring clarity or healing. Be mindful of pride—true connection comes from listening as much as speaking. Leo, your roar inspires when tempered with sincerity. Speak truth with warmth, and you'll leave a lasting impression.

Affirmation & Gratitude

"I speak with clarity and warmth, inspiring others through truth and sincerity."

Leo
28 April 2026

The Moon emphasizes home and family, reminding you to nurture your foundations. Domestic projects or family conversations may need attention. While ambition drives you outward, roots sustain your growth. A peaceful home environment fuels your courage. Today, focus on comfort, stability, and connection with loved ones. Leo, caring for your private world strengthens your public one. Don't overlook the power of love and support close to home.

Affirmation & Gratitude

"I nurture my home and loved ones, honoring the roots of my strength."

Leo
29 April 2026

A Full Moon in Scorpio illuminates your home and career axis, creating a turning point. You may feel torn between personal life and ambition. Emotional revelations could surface, urging you to release old patterns around security or recognition. Balance is key—true success comes when your inner and outer worlds align. Leo, this lunation asks you to let go of what no longer supports your growth, making space for greater achievements.

Affirmation & Gratitude

"I release what no longer serves me, creating balance between home and ambition."

Leo
30 April 2026

After yesterday's Full Moon, emotions may feel raw. Today is about integration and grounding. You may be reviewing recent revelations about home, career, or personal balance. Don't rush into decisions—give yourself time to absorb lessons. Gentle routines, meditation, or nature walks help steady your spirit. Conversations with trusted loved ones may bring perspective. Leo, eclipses and full moons always stir change, but today's calmer energy helps you realign. Trust that clarity is unfolding.

Affirmation & Gratitude

"I allow balance to return, grounding myself as I integrate change."

May 2026

Leo
01 May 2026

The Moon highlights creativity, romance, and self-expression. You may feel playful and inspired, ready to share talents or connect with loved ones. Romantic sparks are likely, or you may simply enjoy laughter and leisure. Professionally, creative ideas thrive—don't dismiss flashes of inspiration. Leo, today is about joy—pure, unapologetic joy. By leaning into play, you replenish the fire that fuels your bigger ambitions. Remember, joy is not frivolous; it's fuel.

Affirmation & Gratitude

"I embrace joy and creativity, letting playfulness restore my fire."

Leo
02 May 2026

The Moon shifts to spotlight health and routines, reminding you to focus on balance. You may feel the need to refine habits, reorganize your schedule, or make adjustments to your daily flow. Productivity comes naturally today, but only when paired with discipline. This isn't punishment—it's empowerment. Leo, your flame shines brighter when fueled by vitality. Take practical steps to support your body and mind; they carry you through every triumph.

Affirmation & Gratitude

"I strengthen myself through balance and discipline, honoring health as the foundation of success."

Leo
03 May 2026

Relationships take priority as Venus brings harmony to your partnerships. Love, affection, and connection flow more easily now. If partnered, enjoy a romantic gesture or meaningful conversation. If single, your magnetism is high—connections may spark unexpectedly. Professionally, collaboration thrives. The universe reminds you today that you don't have to go it alone. Leo, your warmth is irresistible; when you share it with sincerity, relationships blossom beautifully.

Affirmation & Gratitude

"I open my heart to love and partnership, allowing bonds to grow in harmony."

Leo
04 May 2026

Mars energizes your career sector, sparking motivation and drive. You may feel compelled to push forward boldly with projects or chase recognition. This is an excellent day to step up and claim leadership. Just pace yourself—don't let impatience cause tension. Channel ambition into structured action. Leo, your natural confidence paired with this fiery boost makes you unstoppable. Use today to prove your ability not only to shine but to deliver.

Affirmation & Gratitude
"I act boldly and wisely, channeling ambition into steady progress."

Leo
05 May 2026

The Moon draws attention inward, encouraging reflection and solitude. You may crave a break from social or professional demands. Don't ignore this nudge—rest today prepares you for tomorrow's momentum. Intuition is strong; dreams may reveal guidance. Leo, stepping back doesn't dim your light—it strengthens it. Today is about recharging so you can roar with even more power in the days ahead. Honor your inner world as much as the outer.

Affirmation & Gratitude

"I honor stillness, knowing rest renews my strength."

Leo
06 May 2026

Energy surges again as the Moon moves into your sign, amplifying your natural magnetism and vitality. Confidence comes easily, and opportunities to showcase your talents may arise. This is the time to step boldly into visibility—whether in love, work, or creativity. Others are drawn to you; use this attention wisely. Leo, your authentic fire inspires. Today, let yourself enjoy being seen —it's not vanity, it's purpose. You were born to shine.

Affirmation & Gratitude

"I shine authentically, letting my fire inspire others."

Leo
07 May 2026

A New Moon in Taurus lands in your career zone, marking fresh beginnings in ambition, recognition, and long-term goals. You may feel inspired to set new intentions or embark on a project that showcases your leadership. This lunation supports planting seeds of persistence and vision. Don't doubt yourself—your steady efforts will pay off. Leo, the universe is asking you to dream bigger while building practically. Today's intentions can shape months of success.

Affirmation & Gratitude
"I plant bold seeds for my future, trusting steady effort creates lasting success."

Leo
08 May 2026

The Moon highlights partnerships, urging balance and cooperation. Relationships may feel more sensitive, requiring patience and empathy. A partner could seek reassurance, or you may need to compromise. Professionally, teamwork matters—avoid taking full control. Remember, Leo, your fire inspires, but harmony sustains. By honoring others' voices, you create stronger bonds. Today isn't about winning—it's about sharing the light. Lean into love, understanding, and genuine collaboration.

Affirmation & Gratitude

"I honor connection and balance, knowing harmony strengthens all partnerships."

Leo
09 May 2026

Energy turns adventurous as the Moon activates your exploration sector. You may crave travel, learning, or fresh perspectives. Even small actions—reading, exploring a new area, or engaging with diverse people—open doors. Spiritually, this is an excellent day for meditation or philosophical reflection. Leo, your fire expands when you stretch beyond the familiar. Trust curiosity; it leads you to unexpected wisdom and opportunities. Let inspiration guide you toward growth today.

Affirmation & Gratitude
"I embrace curiosity, letting new horizons expand my fire."

Leo
10 May 2026

The Moon highlights your career and ambition, giving you momentum to push forward. Recognition may come, or responsibilities increase. Take initiative—your leadership is noticed. Avoid impatience or arrogance; humility earns long-term respect. This is an excellent day for presenting ideas or showcasing achievements. Leo, your ability to blend charisma with reliability sets you apart. Step into roles where your natural talents inspire others. You're not just seen—you're remembered.

Affirmation & Gratitude
"I lead with confidence and humility, allowing recognition to flow naturally."

Leo
11 May 2026

The cosmos urges inward reflection as the Moon shifts into your spiritual sector. Intuition and sensitivity are heightened. You may feel called to rest, meditate, or release old emotional baggage. Quiet practices today bring clarity and peace. Though your pride prefers the spotlight, Leo, today's magic is subtle. By honoring your inner world, you create balance and renewal. Let go of what no longer serves—it frees space for your light to grow.

Affirmation & Gratitude

"I honor inner peace, trusting release creates space for renewal."

Leo
12 May 2026

The Moon in your sign reignites your confidence and charisma. Energy feels strong—you'll want to move, create, or connect socially. Others notice your magnetism, so it's an ideal time for presentations, dates, or showcasing talents. Be mindful of ego—true leadership inspires rather than overshadows. Leo, today is about standing tall in authenticity. Celebrate yourself unapologetically while making space for others to shine, too. Your roar draws admiration, but your heart earns loyalty.

Affirmation & Gratitude

"I shine authentically, inspiring others with my confidence and heart."

Leo
13 May 2026

Today's focus shifts toward finances and self-worth. You may feel urged to assess spending, income, or investments. Opportunities for abundance may appear, but so may temptations to overspend. Choose wisely—abundance grows when matched with gratitude and discipline. This is also a day to affirm your worth; demand fair recognition for your efforts. Leo, your fire thrives when grounded in self-respect. Claim your value boldly—financial and personal empowerment go hand in hand.

Affirmation & Gratitude

"I honor my worth, making wise choices that build security and abundance."

Leo
14 May 2026

The Moon highlights communication, making this a powerful day for conversations, writing, or sharing ideas. You may feel compelled to speak truthfully about something you've held back, or a key conversation clears the air. Networking and presentations are especially favorable. Be mindful of tone—your roar carries far, so balance strength with warmth. Leo, when you combine honesty with compassion, you leave lasting impact. Today is about speaking from the heart to inspire others.

Affirmation & Gratitude

"I use my words with clarity and compassion, creating truth and connection."

Leo
15 May 2026

Energy shifts toward home and family as the Moon emphasizes your roots. You may feel called to nurture loved ones, handle domestic tasks, or simply enjoy your space. While ambition often pulls you outward, grounding at home restores balance. Pay attention to family conversations—healing and connection are possible. Leo, when your foundation is strong, you stand taller in the world. Today is about cherishing what sustains you privately.

Affirmation & Gratitude

"I honor my home and loved ones, finding strength in my roots."

Leo
16 May 2026

Creativity and romance are emphasized today as the Moon lights your sector of joy and self-expression. This is an excellent time to indulge in hobbies, create art, or enjoy leisure with loved ones. Romantic sparks are likely, and your charisma shines brightly. Professionally, fresh ideas flow easily, so brainstorm or share them. Leo, play is not frivolous—it fuels your brilliance. Today, embrace joy as your greatest tool for inspiration and connection.

Affirmation & Gratitude
"I embrace joy and creativity, letting passion guide my heart."

Leo
17 May 2026

The Moon highlights health, routines, and organization. Productivity is strong today, making it perfect for tackling tasks, refining habits, or addressing wellness. Adjust schedules, clear clutter, or focus on exercise and nutrition. Though it may feel mundane, these efforts build strength for bigger ambitions. Leo, discipline is not your enemy—it is the fuel that sustains your fire. By honoring balance, you give yourself more room to shine.

Affirmation & Gratitude

"I create balance through healthy habits, empowering my body and spirit."

Leo
18 May 2026

Venus enhances your partnership sector, bringing warmth to love and cooperation. If partnered, affection deepens through simple gestures and honesty. Singles may attract someone drawn to your magnetic presence. Professionally, collaboration flows, making team projects easier and more rewarding. Leo, your pride sometimes seeks recognition, but today reminds you that shared success brings deeper satisfaction. Nurture connection with openness—you'll find harmony in both love and work.

Affirmation & Gratitude

"I open my heart to love and cooperation, allowing relationships to thrive."

Leo
19 May 2026

The Sun and Moon align for a Full Moon in Taurus, spotlighting your career. This is a turning point—recognition may arrive, or a project reaches culmination. You may feel torn between ambition and personal life, but clarity comes through balance. Release outdated career goals that no longer inspire you, and focus on what truly lights your fire. Leo, this lunation reminds you success means little without fulfillment. Claim ambitions that align with your heart.

Affirmation & Gratitude

"I align my ambitions with purpose, releasing what no longer serves my fire."

Leo
20 May 2026

Today's energy slows, encouraging reflection after the intensity of the Full Moon. Emotions may feel heavy, but this pause is necessary for clarity. Rest, meditate, or spend time in nature to realign. Avoid forcing outcomes—trust the universe is rearranging pieces behind the scenes. Leo, sometimes your greatest strength is allowing yourself to pause and listen. Quiet wisdom rises when you create space for it. Today is about faith, patience, and inner peace.

Affirmation & Gratitude

"I embrace stillness, trusting the universe to guide my next step."

Leo
21 May 2026

The Sun moves into Gemini, energizing your social and networking zone. For the next month, friendships, community, and collaborations will play a big role. Today, invitations may surface or you could feel drawn to connect with like-minded groups. Your charm makes you magnetic, and people gravitate toward your energy. Leo, your light grows stronger when shared with others—don't isolate. This is a season for building bridges and expanding influence through connection.

Affirmation & Gratitude
"I share my light with others, embracing community and connection."

Leo
22 May 2026

The Moon highlights your inner world, stirring emotions and intuition. You may feel sensitive or crave solitude to process feelings. Pay attention to dreams and synchronicities; they're guiding you. This is not a day for big action, but for preparing inwardly. Leo, sometimes your greatest wisdom comes in quiet reflection. By honoring emotions instead of dismissing them, you strengthen your resilience. Take time to listen to yourself deeply—it's a gift.

Affirmation & Gratitude
"I honor my emotions and intuition, trusting inner wisdom to guide me."

Leo
23 May 2026

The Moon shifts into your sign, bringing vitality, confidence, and visibility. You'll feel more energized and ready to take bold steps. Others notice your charisma easily now, making it a great day for networking, romance, or showcasing your talents. Step forward with authenticity; your natural glow is irresistible. Leo, today is about unapologetically owning your power—shine without shrinking. Remember, when you rise, you inspire others to believe in their own light too.

Affirmation & Gratitude

"I shine unapologetically, inspiring others with my confidence and authenticity."

Leo
24 May 2026

Mars energizes your financial zone, pushing you to take action with money matters. You may feel driven to budget, negotiate, or pursue opportunities for income. Be mindful of impulsive spending—direct fiery energy into building long-term stability. Self-worth is tied to finances now, so recognize your value and demand fair compensation. Leo, when you honor your worth, abundance follows. Today is about bold but practical steps toward prosperity.

Affirmation & Gratitude

"I act wisely with money, honoring my worth and building lasting abundance."

Leo
25 May 2026

The Moon highlights communication, favoring conversations, learning, and writing. Your words carry power today—use them with clarity and warmth. It's a great day for meetings, presentations, or even heart-to-heart talks. Someone's advice may offer unexpected wisdom, so listen closely. Leo, your storytelling is magnetic, but true influence comes when you also hear others. Balance speaking with listening for maximum impact. This energy opens doors through dialogue and shared understanding.

Affirmation & Gratitude

"I use my words with clarity and kindness, creating harmony through communication."

Leo
26 May 2026

Home and family come into focus, urging you to balance ambition with personal roots. Domestic matters may need attention, or you may crave time with loved ones. Don't see this as distraction—it's grounding. Leo, your fire burns brighter when fueled by love and stability at home. Simple acts—sharing meals, tidying space, or heartfelt talks—bring peace. Today reminds you success is sweetest when shared with those closest to you.

Affirmation & Gratitude

"I nurture my home and loved ones, honoring the roots that support me."

Leo
27 May 2026

The Moon lights your creative and romantic zone, bringing inspiration, playfulness, and charm. Joy flows easily, and sparks of romance are likely. Professionally, creative ideas thrive—don't dismiss unusual inspirations. Let your heart lead; when you play, you innovate. Leo, life isn't meant to be all responsibility—your spirit roars when it feels free. Today, laughter, art, and love remind you of your brilliance. Shine through joy—it's your most magnetic energy.

Affirmation & Gratitude

"I embrace joy and creativity, letting my spirit shine freely."

Leo
28 May 2026

The Moon highlights your health and routines, urging you to refine daily habits. You may feel compelled to reorganize your schedule, improve diet, or commit to fitness. Productivity flows when you create structure. Though not glamorous, these adjustments empower your fire long-term. Leo, think of discipline as fuel for your brilliance—it keeps your roar strong. Today is about honoring your body as the vessel that carries your ambitious spirit toward success.

Affirmation & Gratitude

"I honor my body and routines, knowing discipline fuels my fire."

Leo
29 May 2026

Relationships take priority as Venus adds warmth to your partnerships. Romantic moments feel sweeter, and collaborations flow more smoothly. You may feel drawn to share affection, reconcile differences, or simply enjoy companionship. Professionally, team projects thrive under this harmony. Leo, your pride sometimes craves independence, but today reminds you that love and cooperation multiply your joy. Share your heart openly—it's your greatest gift, and it inspires loyalty and connection in return.

Affirmation & Gratitude

"I open my heart to love and harmony, letting connection enrich my life."

Leo
30 May 2026

The Moon energizes your transformation sector, stirring emotions and deeper truths. Conversations about money, intimacy, or vulnerability may feel intense but necessary. Instead of resisting, embrace honesty—you'll emerge stronger. This is also a powerful day to release old habits or limiting beliefs. Transformation isn't always comfortable, but it leads to renewal. Leo, by facing what you've avoided, you claim even more of your authentic power. Courage today plants seeds of freedom.

Affirmation & Gratitude

"I embrace transformation with courage, trusting renewal flows from honesty."

Leo
31 May 2026

The Moon lights your adventure sector, sparking curiosity and inspiration. You may crave travel, learning, or spiritual exploration. Even small steps—like diving into a new book, course, or philosophy—fuel your spirit. Conversations with diverse people may expand your worldview. Leo, your fire grows when you stretch beyond the ordinary. This is a reminder that life is bigger than routine. Feed your curiosity—it's the spark that ignites long-term growth and fulfillment.

Affirmation & Gratitude

"I welcome new horizons, letting curiosity guide my spirit to growth."

June 2026

Leo
01 June 2026

Career matters rise into focus today as the Moon highlights ambition and recognition. You may feel called to push forward with projects or claim the spotlight. Recognition or responsibility may arrive, proving your efforts are noticed. Don't shrink from leadership—this is your moment. Balance confidence with humility, and you'll gain lasting respect. Leo, your natural charisma makes you magnetic, but reliability cements your legacy. Today is about stepping up with grace and power.

Affirmation & Gratitude

"I step into leadership with confidence and humility, earning lasting respect."

Leo
02 June 2026

The cosmos urges inward reflection today. You may crave solitude, meditation, or quiet time away from obligations. Intuition is heightened—listen to subtle guidance from dreams or your inner voice. Though you prefer action, Leo, today's strength comes from stillness. By resting and reflecting, you prepare yourself for bolder moves ahead. Don't resist the pull inward—your fire burns stronger when you give it time to refuel. This is about renewal, not retreat.

Affirmation & Gratitude

"I embrace quiet moments, trusting reflection restores my strength."

Leo
03 June 2026

The Moon moves into your sign, amplifying confidence, charisma, and vitality. You'll feel more visible and ready to take bold action. Others notice your presence easily, making this an ideal day for socializing, romance, or leadership. Step into opportunities—your authenticity is magnetic. Just be mindful of pride; your roar inspires more when it uplifts. Leo, this is a day to celebrate yourself unapologetically while making space for others to shine too.

Affirmation & Gratitude

"I shine authentically, letting my fire inspire and uplift others."

Leo
04 June 2026

The Moon in your sign continues to amplify your charisma and vitality. You may feel bold, eager to take center stage, or ready to push forward with personal goals. This is a strong day for self-expression, romance, and leadership. However, balance is key—don't let pride overpower sensitivity. Leo, your light is magnetic, but it shines brightest when shared with warmth. Use today to inspire others while honoring your authentic self.

Affirmation & Gratitude
"I shine with confidence and warmth, inspiring others through authenticity."

Leo
05 June 2026

The Moon activates your financial zone, urging you to focus on money and self-worth. You may feel driven to budget, negotiate, or explore income opportunities. Temptation to overspend may arise, but discipline leads to stability. This is also about valuing yourself—recognize your worth in personal and professional situations. Leo, abundance starts with self-respect. When you demand fair recognition, the universe mirrors it back. Bold but wise choices create prosperity now.

Affirmation & Gratitude

"I honor my worth and make choices that build lasting abundance."

Leo
06 June 2026

The Moon highlights communication, making today ideal for conversations, teaching, and writing. Your words flow with charisma, drawing others to listen. Important discussions bring clarity, whether personal or professional. Networking thrives, but avoid gossip—it drains your fire. Instead, lean into sincerity and truth. Leo, your roar is powerful, but today it's your thoughtful voice that inspires trust. Share ideas openly, listen closely, and doors will open.

Affirmation & Gratitude
"I speak with clarity and sincerity, creating connection through truth."

Leo
07 June 2026

Home and family take priority today as the Moon shifts your focus inward. Domestic projects, family conversations, or simply creating comfort feel important. This isn't distraction—it's foundation. By nurturing your home, you fuel your external success. Emotional conversations may bring healing, so listen with an open heart. Leo, your pride shines in the world, but roots sustain your roar. Today, cherish those who give you love and stability.

Affirmation & Gratitude

"I nurture my home and loved ones, honoring the foundation of my strength."

Leo
08 June 2026

The Moon lights your creativity and romance sector, bringing playful and inspired energy. You may feel drawn to art, hobbies, or leisure that fuels joy. Romantic sparks could surprise you, or relationships may feel lighter and more affectionate. Professionally, fresh ideas shine—don't dismiss inspirations. Leo, joy is your natural state, and today reminds you that play fuels success. Lean into fun, and let creativity guide your heart.

Affirmation & Gratitude

"I embrace joy and creativity, letting play fuel my spirit."

Leo
09 June 2026

Productivity peaks as the Moon emphasizes health and routines. You may feel driven to reorganize, clear clutter, or refine habits. Focus on wellness and consistency. Though routine may feel mundane, Leo, it strengthens your fire for bigger ambitions. Discipline empowers freedom, not restricts it. Today is about small steps that yield powerful results over time. Choose habits that support vitality, and your roar will echo even louder tomorrow.

Affirmation & Gratitude

"I strengthen myself through balance and healthy habits, empowering my future."

Leo
10 June 2026

Venus brings harmony to your partnerships, highlighting love, affection, and cooperation. Relationships feel smoother, with opportunities for romance or deeper connection. Professionally, teamwork thrives as collaboration becomes more natural. If misunderstandings linger, this is the perfect day to heal them. Leo, your pride sometimes resists compromise, but vulnerability strengthens bonds. Let your warmth guide you, and watch connections flourish beautifully. Today is about love in all its forms—cherish it.

Affirmation & Gratitude

"I open my heart to love and cooperation, allowing relationships to thrive."

Leo
11 June 2026

The Moon highlights your transformation zone, stirring deeper emotions and insights. Matters around intimacy, trust, or shared resources may surface. Though intense, these conversations bring healing if faced with honesty. Don't fear vulnerability—it builds strength. You may also feel compelled to release habits or beliefs that no longer serve. Transformation is rarely comfortable, but Leo, you thrive when you face challenges head-on. Embrace change; it clears space for greater authenticity and freedom.

Affirmation & Gratitude

"I embrace transformation with courage, knowing release creates renewal."

Leo
12 June 2026

The Moon moves into your exploration zone, inspiring curiosity and adventure. You may crave travel, study, or experiences that expand your worldview. Even small actions—reading, journaling, or engaging with different perspectives—ignite inspiration. Spiritually, today offers breakthroughs in wisdom if you stay open. Leo, your fire grows brighter when fueled by learning and new horizons. Say yes to opportunities that stretch your boundaries; growth is waiting just outside your comfort zone.

Affirmation & Gratitude

"I embrace curiosity, letting new horizons expand my spirit."

Leo
13 June 2026

The Moon activates your career zone, spotlighting ambition, recognition, and responsibility. Opportunities may arise to showcase leadership or gain acknowledgment for your efforts. This is a day to step forward boldly—your charisma naturally attracts notice. Balance confidence with humility, and you'll gain lasting respect. Leo, today's cosmic energy supports you in building your legacy. Take one concrete step toward long-term goals, and trust your fire to carry you forward.

Affirmation & Gratitude
"I step into leadership with confidence and humility, building my legacy."

Leo
14 June 2026

The Moon moves into your spiritual and inner world, urging rest and reflection. You may feel drawn to solitude, meditation, or journaling. Dreams or intuition bring guidance—pay attention. Though your pride prefers action, Leo, today is about renewal through stillness. This pause isn't weakness—it's wisdom. Recharge your inner fire so you can shine brighter tomorrow. Balance is the key to sustaining your energy across the long journey.

Affirmation & Gratitude

"I honor stillness, knowing rest restores my strength and clarity."

Leo
15 June 2026

The Moon enters your sign, reigniting confidence, vitality, and charisma. Energy feels high—you'll want to take bold steps forward. Visibility increases, making this a great day for networking, romance, or creative expression. Others are drawn to your magnetism, but remember: true leadership uplifts rather than overshadows. Leo, when you shine authentically, you inspire others to do the same. Today is about celebrating yourself while leaving room for others' light too.

Affirmation & Gratitude

"I shine authentically, inspiring others through my confidence and warmth."

Leo
16 June 2026

The Moon highlights finances and self-worth, urging you to focus on resources. You may feel compelled to budget, negotiate, or demand recognition for your efforts. Abundance grows when paired with gratitude and wise decisions. Don't let pride push you into overspending—security comes from grounded choices. Leo, remember wealth is more than money—it's self-respect. Today's actions can build prosperity if you stand tall in your value and act wisely.

Affirmation & Gratitude

"I honor my worth, making choices that create lasting abundance."

Leo
17 June 2026

Communication takes center stage today as the Moon energizes your networking and learning zone. Your words carry weight and charm, making this a perfect day for teaching, presenting, or simply sharing ideas. Be mindful of listening as much as speaking—insight comes from dialogue. A casual conversation may lead to opportunity. Leo, your roar inspires, but today it's your thoughtful voice that draws admiration. Use your words to connect and uplift.

Affirmation & Gratitude

"I use my voice with clarity and warmth, creating connection and opportunity."

Leo
18 June 2026

The Moon highlights home and family, reminding you to ground yourself. Domestic matters may need attention, or you may crave comfort and stability. A heartfelt conversation with loved ones brings healing, while tending to your space restores balance. Leo, your fire burns brightest when your roots are steady. Today's lesson is that success isn't just external—it begins with the foundation you build in private. Create peace at home, and everything else flows smoother.

Affirmation & Gratitude

"I nurture my home and loved ones, knowing strong roots sustain my fire."

Leo
19 June 2026

Creativity and romance are amplified as the Moon lights your joy sector. This is a perfect day for art, hobbies, or playful connections. Romantic sparks are likely, and relationships feel lighter. Professionally, creative projects thrive, and fresh ideas emerge. Leo, your magnetism soars when you let yourself have fun—joy is your natural fuel. Today reminds you that embracing play isn't distraction, it's nourishment for your spirit and inspiration for your ambitions.

Affirmation & Gratitude

"I embrace joy and creativity, letting play fuel my spirit."

Leo
20 June 2026

The Moon emphasizes routines, health, and organization. You may feel driven to refine habits, clear clutter, or reset priorities. Productivity flows naturally, but balance effort with rest. Wellness choices made today set you up for long-term vitality. Leo, though structure may feel limiting, it's actually empowering—it fuels your fiery ambitions. Take small, consistent steps to strengthen your foundation, and you'll feel unstoppable. Today is about honoring your body as your true temple.

Affirmation & Gratitude

"I strengthen myself with healthy routines, creating balance and energy for success."

Leo
21 June 2026

The Sun enters Cancer, shifting your focus inward for the coming month. This is a spiritual and reflective season, encouraging you to process emotions, heal, and rest before your birthday cycle begins. Today, you may feel more sensitive, but that sensitivity carries wisdom. Intuition is strong—pay attention to subtle nudges. Leo, now is the time to retreat slightly so you can recharge. Stillness will prepare you for the bold leaps ahead.

Affirmation & Gratitude

"I honor reflection and healing, trusting rest prepares me for renewal."

Leo
22 June 2026

The Moon emphasizes partnerships, bringing relationships into focus. Romantic bonds may deepen, or professional collaborations strengthen. Balance is the theme—avoid dominance and seek harmony. If tensions have lingered, today is perfect for resolving them with honesty and kindness. Leo, your pride sometimes craves control, but real power is found in cooperation. Shared strength always outshines solitary success. Today, nurture your connections—they are the mirrors that reflect your light more brightly.

Affirmation & Gratitude

"I value cooperation and balance, allowing relationships to flourish with love."

Leo
23 June 2026

The Moon highlights exploration, adventure, and higher learning. You may feel restless, eager to experience more of life beyond routine. Travel, study, or spiritual pursuits are favored. Even small actions—like diving into new knowledge or engaging with fresh perspectives—bring joy. Leo, your fire expands when you stretch beyond comfort zones. This is a reminder that curiosity keeps you vibrant. Let today be about saying yes to opportunities that fuel growth.

Affirmation & Gratitude

"I embrace curiosity and exploration, letting new horizons expand my spirit."

Leo
24 June 2026

The Moon activates your career sector, spotlighting ambition and recognition. You may feel pressure to perform, but also the thrill of leadership opportunities. A superior may notice your efforts, or you may feel inspired to take bold steps toward goals. Balance pride with humility—respect grows from both. Leo, today is about demonstrating reliability alongside charisma. Show the world you're not only a star, but also a steady, trustworthy leader.

Affirmation & Gratitude
"I lead with confidence and humility, building respect through action."

Leo
25 June 2026

The Moon encourages rest and reflection, pulling you inward after recent career demands. You may crave solitude, journaling, or meditation. This is not a day to force outcomes—clarity will come through stillness. Dreams may feel especially vivid, carrying guidance. Leo, though you thrive in the spotlight, honoring your inner world is equally important. Today's pause gives your spirit room to recharge, preparing you for bolder moves ahead. Treat rest as fuel, not weakness.

Affirmation & Gratitude

"I honor rest and reflection, trusting stillness restores my strength."

Leo
26 June 2026

The Moon moves into your sign, reigniting vitality and confidence. You'll feel eager to step forward with fresh ideas, romance, or creativity. Others notice your glow easily—your charisma is magnetic now. This is a great day to showcase talents, pursue opportunities, or simply enjoy admiration. Be mindful of pride; your leadership shines brightest when paired with generosity. Leo, the world is ready for your roar—share it unapologetically but with heart.

Affirmation & Gratitude

"I shine with confidence and generosity, inspiring others with my authenticity."

Leo
27 June 2026

The Moon emphasizes finances and self-worth, encouraging reflection on money habits and personal value. You may feel driven to budget, plan, or ask for recognition at work. Abundance flows when paired with gratitude and wisdom. Avoid impulsive purchases; instead, focus on building stability. Leo, true wealth comes not just from material success but from honoring your worth. Today, demand fairness in all areas of life—it affirms your value to the universe.

Affirmation & Gratitude

"I honor my worth, making wise choices that attract lasting abundance."

Leo
28 June 2026

The Moon highlights communication, making today ideal for conversations, learning, and networking. Your words carry extra influence, so use them with care. Professionally, pitches or presentations thrive; personally, heartfelt talks bring healing or inspiration. A casual chat could open doors—stay open. Leo, your roar is powerful, but your thoughtful words inspire deeper trust. Balance speaking with listening, and your influence will ripple far. Connection is your key to opportunity today.

Affirmation & Gratitude
"I speak with clarity and kindness, creating harmony and opportunity through dialogue."

Leo
29 June 2026

Home and family matters take center stage as the Moon shifts focus to your roots. Domestic projects, family conversations, or simply enjoying time at home bring comfort. This is a chance to strengthen bonds and create peace. Leo, though ambition calls, nurturing your foundation ensures you can soar higher. Success feels more meaningful when shared with loved ones. Today, prioritize the spaces and people that make you feel grounded and loved.

Affirmation & Gratitude

"I nurture my home and loved ones, honoring the roots that sustain me."

Leo
30 June 2026

The Moon lights your creative and playful sector, boosting joy, romance, and inspiration. You may feel drawn to hobbies, art, or leisure activities that spark delight. Romantic sparks are likely, and relationships feel fun. Professionally, creative solutions emerge—don't ignore flashes of inspiration. Leo, joy isn't frivolous; it's essential to your brilliance. By embracing play and creativity, you fuel your inner fire and attract admiration effortlessly. Shine through fun today—it's magnetic.

Affirmation & Gratitude

"I embrace joy and creativity, letting passion fuel my spirit."

July 2026

Leo
01 July 2026

The Moon emphasizes health, routines, and productivity. You may feel motivated to refine daily habits, clear clutter, or organize schedules. This is a powerful day for discipline and structure. Though routine may feel restrictive, it supports your fiery ambitions. Leo, discipline is not the opposite of freedom—it's what sustains it. Small, consistent steps taken today will build lasting strength and energy for tomorrow's achievements. Focus on creating systems that empower you.

Affirmation & Gratitude

"I strengthen my routines with discipline, fueling freedom and vitality."

Leo
02 July 2026

The Moon highlights partnerships, bringing relationships to the forefront. You may feel called to nurture romance, strengthen business ties, or resolve conflicts. Cooperation flows more easily if you set aside pride and listen with empathy. Compromise isn't weakness—it's wisdom. Professional collaborations can also thrive, especially if you share credit generously. Leo, your natural warmth inspires loyalty, but today requires balance between leading and listening. Strong bonds now set the tone for long-term harmony.

Affirmation & Gratitude

"I honor balance in relationships, knowing cooperation creates lasting strength."

Leo
03 July 2026

The Moon shifts into your exploration zone, sparking curiosity and a desire for adventure. You may crave travel, learning, or new experiences. Even small actions—exploring a book, a class, or a cultural event—can inspire growth. Spiritually, breakthroughs are possible if you remain open. Leo, your fire grows brighter when you stretch beyond comfort zones. Say yes to discovery today—these sparks may light a path toward long-term expansion.

Affirmation & Gratitude

"I embrace curiosity and adventure, letting new experiences fuel my spirit."

Leo
04 July 2026

The Moon activates your career sector, bringing visibility, ambition, and leadership opportunities. Recognition is possible, or responsibilities may increase. This is your moment to step forward confidently and prove your abilities. Balance pride with humility—true respect is earned through action. Leo, today reminds you that your roar isn't just for show—it inspires trust when backed with substance. Show up with reliability, and doors to lasting success will open.

Affirmation & Gratitude

"I lead with confidence and humility, earning recognition through action."

Leo
05 July 2026

A quieter energy flows as the Moon moves into your spiritual sector. You may crave solitude, reflection, or intuitive practices. Dreams or inner whispers carry guidance—pay attention. Though your pride thrives in activity, today asks you to slow down. Leo, rest isn't laziness—it's renewal. By honoring your inner world, you prepare yourself for bolder moves ahead. Recharge your fire; stillness is your ally, not your enemy.

Affirmation & Gratitude

"I honor stillness, trusting reflection restores my fire."

Leo
06 July 2026

The Moon enters your sign, reigniting vitality, charm, and courage. Energy flows easily, and others are drawn to your presence. This is a perfect day to take bold steps toward personal goals, romance, or creativity. Your charisma makes you magnetic, but remember—true leadership uplifts others too. Leo, when you shine authentically, you give permission for others to do the same. Celebrate your confidence unapologetically today while sharing the stage generously.

Affirmation & Gratitude

"I shine authentically, inspiring others through my light and warmth."

Leo
07 July 2026

The Moon highlights your finances and self-worth, urging you to reflect on resources. You may feel motivated to budget, save, or negotiate fair pay. Abundance grows when grounded in gratitude and wise choices. Avoid impulsive purchases—focus on building stability instead. Leo, wealth isn't just money; it's the respect you hold for yourself. Demand recognition where deserved, and align spending with values. Financial empowerment strengthens your freedom to pursue passions.

Affirmation & Gratitude

"I value myself and manage resources wisely, creating lasting abundance."

Leo
08 July 2026

Communication takes center stage as the Moon activates your networking and learning zone. Your words carry impact today—whether in presentations, casual chats, or heartfelt talks. Be mindful of tone; balance strength with kindness. A conversation could spark opportunity, or an idea may take root that shapes your path forward. Leo, your storytelling inspires, but true influence comes from listening as much as speaking. Use your voice thoughtfully—it's your most magnetic tool.

Affirmation & Gratitude

"I communicate with clarity and kindness, inspiring connection and opportunity."

Leo
09 July 2026

The Moon highlights home and family, urging you to reconnect with your roots. Domestic matters may need attention, or you might feel drawn to create comfort in your living space. Family conversations bring opportunities for healing and understanding. Leo, while your pride often craves the spotlight, today reminds you that your power also comes from your foundation. Nurture your private world; strong roots make your roar echo louder in the outside world.

Affirmation & Gratitude

"I nurture my home and loved ones, honoring the foundation that supports me."

Leo
10 July 2026

The Moon emphasizes creativity, romance, and joy. You may feel inspired to pursue hobbies, art, or leisure that fuels passion. Romantic sparks are strong—whether deepening an existing relationship or attracting new interest. Professionally, creativity shines, and your ideas captivate others. Leo, joy is your natural state, and when you embrace play, you ignite inspiration in yourself and those around you. Today is about celebrating life's pleasures unapologetically.

Affirmation & Gratitude

"I embrace joy and creativity, letting passion fuel my spirit."

Leo
11 July 2026

The Moon moves into your health and routines sector, encouraging discipline and structure. You may feel motivated to refine daily habits, clear clutter, or focus on wellness. Productivity flows when you balance ambition with self-care. Leo, your pride thrives in big achievements, but today's gift lies in the small steps that sustain long-term success. Consistency is your ally; use today to build habits that keep your fire burning bright.

Affirmation & Gratitude

"I honor healthy routines, creating balance that sustains my fire."

Leo
12 July 2026

The Moon energizes your partnership sector, placing relationships in the spotlight. You may feel called to nurture romance, strengthen teamwork, or resolve conflicts. Balance between giving and receiving is key—avoid letting pride block vulnerability. Professionally, collaborations thrive when you share credit generously. Leo, your warmth attracts loyalty, but true strength lies in cooperation. Today is about strengthening bonds through love, patience, and openness.

Affirmation & Gratitude

"I honor balance in relationships, creating harmony through love and cooperation."

Leo
13 July 2026

The Moon lights up your exploration and adventure zone, stirring restlessness and curiosity. You may crave new experiences, travel, or learning. Even small steps—reading a book, starting a course, or engaging with new perspectives—expand your worldview. Spiritually, this is an excellent day for meditation or reflection. Leo, your fire thrives when fed with knowledge and inspiration. Stretch beyond the familiar; today is about growing your spirit through discovery.

Affirmation & Gratitude
"I welcome new horizons, letting curiosity fuel my growth."

Leo
14 July 2026

A Full Moon in Capricorn highlights health, work, and routines. This is a turning point—habits that no longer serve you must be released. You may realize it's time to prioritize wellness or restructure your schedule for balance. Professionally, projects may peak, demanding completion or recognition. Leo, success comes not just from big leaps but from steady discipline. Today's Full Moon reminds you to align daily choices with long-term vitality and purpose.

Affirmation & Gratitude

"I release old habits and embrace routines that support my strength and success."

Leo
15 July 2026

After the intensity of yesterday's Full Moon, today offers calmer energy for integration. You may feel reflective, reviewing insights about health, work, and balance. Don't push yourself too hard—allow time to absorb lessons. Gentle routines, meditation, or grounding practices will help realign your focus. Leo, honoring balance doesn't dim your fire—it strengthens it. Today is about finding peace in the pause, preparing you for the next bold step forward.

Affirmation & Gratitude

"I honor balance and reflection, trusting stillness strengthens my fire."

Leo
16 July 2026

The Moon moves into your career sector, spotlighting ambition, recognition, and progress. Opportunities to showcase leadership may arrive, or you may feel compelled to push projects forward with determination. Your natural charisma draws attention, but humility ensures respect. Leo, today is about proving that your roar is backed by reliability and effort. Recognition flows when others see your consistent dedication. Take one bold but grounded step toward your long-term goals today.

Affirmation & Gratitude
"I lead with confidence and humility, proving my strength through action."

Leo
17 July 2026

The Moon shifts into your spiritual sector, pulling you inward for rest and reflection. Intuition is heightened—dreams or synchronicities may bring guidance. You may feel drained if you push too hard, so embrace stillness instead. Leo, your pride often wants action, but wisdom comes from balance. Today offers subtle insights that prepare you for greater leaps ahead. Honor the quiet, for it carries truths your fire alone cannot reveal.

Affirmation & Gratitude
"I honor stillness, trusting my intuition to guide me."

Leo
18 July 2026

The Moon enters your sign, reigniting energy, confidence, and visibility. You'll feel ready to take center stage, whether socially, romantically, or professionally. Others notice your magnetism easily—don't shy away. This is a day for bold action and self-expression. Just remember: true leadership inspires rather than dominates. Leo, shine authentically, and you'll uplift others while claiming your rightful place in the spotlight. Celebrate your uniqueness unapologetically today—it's your gift to the world.

Affirmation & Gratitude

"I shine authentically, inspiring others through my confidence and warmth."

Leo
19 July 2026

The Moon highlights your financial zone, urging focus on money matters and self-worth. You may feel motivated to budget, review expenses, or request recognition for your value. Avoid impulsive spending—direct energy toward building stability. Abundance flows when paired with wisdom and gratitude. Leo, true wealth is more than material—it's the confidence to honor your worth. Demand fairness today, and align choices with values for lasting security and empowerment.

Affirmation & Gratitude

"I honor my worth, making wise choices that attract abundance."

Leo
20 July 2026

The Moon energizes communication, making today ideal for important conversations, writing, or networking. Your words flow with clarity and magnetism, inspiring others easily. A discussion may bring resolution or open unexpected opportunities. Professionally, presentations thrive; personally, heartfelt talks heal. Leo, your roar inspires when paired with sincerity. Balance speaking with listening, and your influence will ripple outward. Today is about using your voice as a tool for truth and connection.

Affirmation & Gratitude
"I use my words with sincerity and warmth, creating harmony through communication."

Leo
21 July 2026

The Moon emphasizes home and family, urging you to focus on roots and stability. Domestic matters may require attention, or you may feel drawn to nurture loved ones. This grounding energy balances your ambitious drive. Simple gestures—sharing meals, tidying, or heartfelt conversations—restore peace. Leo, though you crave the spotlight, strong foundations keep you steady. Today is about cherishing the spaces and people that sustain you behind the scenes.

Affirmation & Gratitude

"I nurture my home and loved ones, honoring the roots that sustain me."

Leo
22 July 2026

The Sun enters your sign, kicking off your birthday season with fire and vitality. Energy surges, and you'll feel more confident, visible, and eager to set intentions for the year ahead. This is your cosmic reset, Leo—a chance to claim the spotlight unapologetically. Set bold goals that align with your heart. Your charisma attracts opportunities now; use it wisely. Today marks the start of a cycle where your roar is unstoppable.

Affirmation & Gratitude

"I celebrate my light, setting bold intentions for the year ahead."

Leo
23 July 2026

The Moon lights your joy and creativity sector, sparking playfulness and romance. You'll feel inspired to indulge in hobbies, art, or leisure that excites you. Romantic connections may feel lighter and more affectionate. Professionally, fresh ideas flow easily—don't dismiss sudden sparks of inspiration. Leo, joy isn't a distraction; it's fuel for your fire. When you embrace fun unapologetically, your magnetism expands, attracting admiration and opportunities alike. Today is about celebrating life's pleasures.

Affirmation & Gratitude

"I embrace joy and creativity, letting passion and play fuel my spirit."

Leo
24 July 2026

The Moon emphasizes health and routines, urging focus on balance. You may feel motivated to reorganize your schedule, refine habits, or tackle tasks you've been avoiding. Wellness choices—exercise, rest, nutrition—are especially powerful now. Leo, though you crave grand achievements, success is built on consistency. Today's gift lies in small, sustainable steps that keep your energy high. Think of discipline as empowerment; it strengthens your roar for future triumphs.

Affirmation & Gratitude

"I honor balance and discipline, creating habits that sustain my fire."

Leo
25 July 2026

The Moon highlights relationships, bringing harmony and cooperation into focus. Romantic bonds may deepen through meaningful conversations, while professional partnerships flow more smoothly. If tensions have lingered, today offers a chance to resolve them with empathy. Leo, your pride sometimes resists compromise, but real strength is found in balance. Shared success always feels sweeter. Use today to nurture connection—both love and loyalty thrive under your generous warmth.

Affirmation & Gratitude

"I honor love and cooperation, creating harmony in my relationships."

Leo
26 July 2026

The Moon enters your exploration sector, sparking curiosity and a thirst for adventure. You may crave travel, learning, or experiences that stretch your perspective. Even small steps—like reading, studying, or meeting someone new—bring inspiration. Spiritually, today may offer breakthroughs if you stay open. Leo, your fire thrives when you explore beyond comfort zones. Feed your curiosity; it's the spark that ignites long-term growth and wisdom.

Affirmation & Gratitude
"I embrace new horizons, letting curiosity expand my spirit."

Leo
27 July 2026

The Moon highlights your career, ambition, and recognition. You may feel ready to step into leadership or claim acknowledgment for your work. A superior may notice your efforts, or an opportunity could arise. Balance pride with humility—true leadership is earned. Leo, today is about proving your roar has substance. Consistency and dedication shine as brightly as charisma. Step forward confidently—your legacy is built one bold choice at a time.

Affirmation & Gratitude
"I step confidently into leadership, blending ambition with humility."

Leo
28 July 2026

Today's Moon emphasizes your spiritual sector, pulling you inward for rest and reflection. Intuition is heightened—dreams, synchronicities, or inner whispers carry messages. Avoid overexertion; recharge instead. This pause isn't laziness, it's wisdom. Leo, your pride prefers visibility, but growth requires balance. By honoring your inner world, you prepare yourself for brighter expression tomorrow. Quiet time today plants seeds of renewal and strength for the weeks ahead.

Affirmation & Gratitude
"I honor stillness and intuition, knowing reflection strengthens my fire."

Leo
29 July 2026

The Moon enters your sign, boosting confidence, vitality, and charm. You'll feel more visible and ready to take bold action. Opportunities to showcase talents, pursue romance, or enjoy social life appear easily. Others are drawn to your natural glow—use it to inspire rather than overshadow. Leo, your authentic roar is irresistible when paired with generosity. Today, celebrate yourself unapologetically—you were born to shine.

Affirmation & Gratitude

"I shine authentically, inspiring others with my warmth and confidence."

Leo
30 July 2026

The Moon emphasizes finances and self-worth, urging you to review money habits and align spending with values. You may feel called to budget, negotiate, or demand recognition for your efforts. Avoid impulsive purchases; instead, focus on creating stability. Abundance grows when gratitude and wisdom guide your choices. Leo, true wealth is more than material—it's the confidence to honor your worth. Today, empower yourself by acting in alignment with your values.

Affirmation & Gratitude

"I honor my worth and manage resources with wisdom, creating lasting abundance."

Leo
31 July 2026

The Moon activates communication, making this a powerful day for speaking, writing, and connecting. Your words hold weight—use them wisely. Conversations may bring clarity, healing, or even opportunity. Networking is favored, but be mindful not to dominate. Leo, your roar inspires when tempered with sincerity. Today is about using your voice to connect, uplift, and inspire. Listen deeply as much as you speak; dialogue creates breakthroughs.

Affirmation & Gratitude
"I use my words with clarity and kindness, creating harmony through communication."

August 2026

Leo
01 August 2026

A New Moon in Leo opens a powerful new chapter for you. This is your cosmic reset, a time to set bold intentions for the year ahead. What do you truly want to create, attract, or embody? The universe hands you the pen to write your next story. Leo, step into your power unapologetically. Dream big, act bravely, and claim the spotlight. Your season is here—ignite it with courage and joy.

Affirmation & Gratitude

"I set bold intentions, trusting my light to guide a powerful new chapter."

Leo
02 August 2026

The Moon highlights home and family, grounding you after yesterday's fiery New Moon. Domestic projects, conversations, or quiet time with loved ones restore balance. Your ambitions are strong, but roots sustain wings. Leo, today reminds you that success is sweeter when shared with those who support you. Nurture your private world; it fuels your public victories. Healing family ties or creating comfort at home strengthens your foundation for the year ahead.

Affirmation & Gratitude

"I nurture my home and family, honoring the foundation of my strength."

Leo
03 August 2026

The Moon lights your creative and romantic sector, amplifying inspiration, joy, and magnetism. You may feel drawn to hobbies, art, or playful connections. Romance feels exciting, and your charisma shines brightly. Professionally, creative breakthroughs are possible—don't dismiss unusual ideas. Leo, when you embrace play and passion, opportunities flow naturally. Today is about celebrating life unapologetically and letting joy fuel your brilliance. Shine through fun—it's your most magnetic energy.

Affirmation & Gratitude
"I embrace joy and creativity, letting passion inspire my brilliance."

Leo
04 August 2026

The Moon emphasizes health, routines, and productivity. You'll feel motivated to organize, refine habits, or tackle tasks you've delayed. Though not glamorous, these actions empower your long-term goals. Leo, discipline is your ally—it sustains your fire when ambition runs high. Today is about honoring balance and consistency. By strengthening your routines, you create the foundation needed to shine in larger arenas. Small steps today pave the way for major victories tomorrow.

Affirmation & Gratitude

"I honor balance and discipline, creating habits that sustain my fire."

Leo
05 August 2026

Relationships take center stage as Venus emphasizes love, harmony, and cooperation. Bonds may feel more affectionate, and collaborations flow smoothly. If tensions linger, this is the perfect day to heal them through empathy and kindness. Professionally, teamwork thrives. Leo, your pride sometimes resists compromise, but today reminds you that cooperation multiplies success. Your warmth is your greatest gift—share it openly to create harmony in both love and work.

Affirmation & Gratitude
"I open my heart to love and cooperation, allowing relationships to thrive."

Leo
06 August 2026

The Moon highlights your exploration zone, sparking curiosity and adventure. You may crave travel, study, or simply a break from routine. Even small actions—like diving into a new subject or exploring a different perspective—expand your spirit. Spiritually, breakthroughs are possible if you remain open. Leo, your fire grows brighter when fueled by discovery. Today is about stretching beyond the familiar to welcome growth. Say yes to experiences that awaken inspiration and courage.

Affirmation & Gratitude
"I embrace curiosity and new horizons, letting discovery expand my fire."

Leo
07 August 2026

The Moon activates your career zone, bringing visibility and ambition. Recognition may come, or responsibilities increase, showcasing your leadership. Step forward with confidence, but temper pride with humility. Today is about proving your roar has substance—consistency earns respect. A mentor or superior may notice your dedication, offering opportunities. Leo, you're building a legacy with every action. Today's focus is about showing reliability alongside charisma. Trust your efforts to carry you forward.

Affirmation & Gratitude

"I step confidently into leadership, blending passion with reliability."

Leo
08 August 2026

A quieter energy flows as the Moon enters your spiritual sector, urging rest, reflection, and intuitive practices. Dreams or synchronicities may carry messages—pay attention. You may crave solitude or feel drained if you overextend. Leo, though you thrive on attention, today is about honoring your inner fire. Stillness is where wisdom grows. Allow yourself time to recharge—you'll emerge stronger, clearer, and more centered. Trust that retreat is part of your power.

Affirmation & Gratitude
"I honor stillness and intuition, knowing reflection strengthens my spirit."

Leo
09 August 2026

The Moon moves into your sign, boosting charisma, vitality, and confidence. You'll feel visible, magnetic, and eager to act on your goals. Others notice you more easily—use this spotlight wisely. Romance and creativity are also heightened. Leo, this is your moment to roar unapologetically, but remember: the greatest leaders inspire others to shine too. Today is about celebrating yourself authentically while sharing warmth with those around you.

Affirmation & Gratitude

"I shine authentically, inspiring others with my light and generosity."

Leo
10 August 2026

The Moon highlights your finances and self-worth, encouraging reflection on money habits and value. You may feel motivated to budget, save, or request recognition for your contributions. Abundance grows when paired with wisdom and gratitude. Avoid impulsive spending—focus instead on building long-term stability. Leo, true wealth isn't just financial—it's knowing your worth and acting accordingly. Stand tall in your value, and the world will mirror it back.

Affirmation & Gratitude

"I honor my worth, making wise choices that create lasting abundance."

Leo
11 August 2026

The Moon energizes communication, making today perfect for speaking, writing, or networking. Your words carry influence—professionally, proposals or meetings thrive; personally, heartfelt talks bring healing or clarity. Balance confidence with listening, as insights may come through others. Leo, your roar is powerful, but it's your thoughtful voice that builds bridges. Today is about connection, inspiration, and opportunities born through dialogue. Share your truth with warmth, and doors will open.

Affirmation & Gratitude

"I communicate with clarity and kindness, creating harmony and opportunity."

Leo
12 August 2026

The Moon shifts focus to home and family, reminding you of the importance of roots and stability. Domestic matters may need care, or you may crave time with loved ones. Simple acts—sharing meals, cleaning, or heartfelt conversations—bring peace. Leo, while ambition calls, your foundation sustains your fire. Today, prioritize those who support you unconditionally. Strong roots give you the courage to grow higher in the outside world.

Affirmation & Gratitude

"I nurture my home and loved ones, honoring the roots of my strength."

Leo
13 August 2026

The Moon highlights your creative and romantic zone, sparking joy, passion, and inspiration. You may feel drawn to hobbies, art, or activities that let you express yourself. Romance feels vibrant, and playful energy flows easily into relationships. Professionally, fresh ideas break through routine thinking. Leo, creativity isn't a luxury—it's how your soul roars. Today is about honoring the spark that makes you unique. Celebrate joy unapologetically; it fuels both your heart and ambitions.

Affirmation & Gratitude
"I embrace joy and creativity, letting my passion inspire my world."

Leo
14 August 2026

The Moon emphasizes health, routines, and productivity, urging you to refine daily habits. You may feel motivated to tackle lingering tasks, improve organization, or commit to wellness goals. Though routine may feel dull, discipline strengthens your vitality and prepares you for bigger leaps. Leo, remember: success isn't built in one roar—it's sustained by daily choices. Today, every small act of balance contributes to your long-term fire and stability.

Affirmation & Gratitude

"I create balance with healthy routines, fueling my strength and freedom."

Leo
15 August 2026

Relationships take focus as the Moon energizes your partnership sector. Connections may feel more affectionate, or a conversation could bring clarity. Collaborations flow smoothly if you value balance and cooperation. Avoid pride-driven conflicts—compromise strengthens bonds. Leo, you shine brightly, but today is about sharing light equally. Love and teamwork thrive when nurtured with openness and respect. Use today to deepen bonds and remind others why they value your warmth.

Affirmation & Gratitude

"I honor love and cooperation, allowing relationships to grow in harmony."

Leo
16 August 2026

The Moon moves into your exploration zone, sparking curiosity and a need for growth. You may crave travel, study, or spiritual exploration. Even small steps—reading, journaling, or seeking new perspectives—bring fulfillment. Leo, your fire thrives when you step beyond routine into new horizons. Today, life asks you to say yes to discovery. Inspiration is waiting in unfamiliar places—trust that your spirit grows through adventure.

Affirmation & Gratitude
"I embrace curiosity and exploration, letting new horizons expand my fire."

Leo
17 August 2026

The Moon highlights your career sector, bringing visibility and ambition. Leadership opportunities may surface, or recognition for your work could arrive. Step confidently into the spotlight, but avoid arrogance—humility makes victories last longer. Leo, today is about showing substance alongside charisma. Consistency, effort, and authenticity secure your legacy. Claim your role proudly, and let your reliability prove your roar carries true weight. Opportunities today may ripple far into the future.

Affirmation & Gratitude

"I step confidently into leadership, proving my strength through action."

Leo
18 August 2026

The Moon emphasizes reflection and spiritual renewal, slowing your pace after career demands. Intuition is heightened—pay attention to dreams, synchronicities, or inner whispers. You may feel called to rest or retreat from obligations. Leo, your pride often resists slowing down, but wisdom lives in stillness. Today's insights help you prepare for bigger moves later this month. Honor your inner world—it is the quiet fire that fuels your roar.

Affirmation & Gratitude

"I honor stillness and intuition, trusting reflection strengthens my spirit."

Leo
19 August 2026

The Moon enters your sign, amplifying confidence, charisma, and visibility. You'll feel vibrant and ready to take bold steps forward. Opportunities in love, career, or creativity flow naturally—your magnetism is undeniable. Be mindful of ego; inspire others by sharing the spotlight. Leo, this is a day to celebrate yourself authentically while reminding others that leadership uplifts. Your roar is heard today—make it a song of courage, joy, and generosity.

Affirmation & Gratitude

"I shine authentically, inspiring others with my light and warmth."

Leo
20 August 2026

The Moon highlights finances and self-worth, urging you to reflect on your relationship with money and personal value. You may feel inspired to budget, negotiate, or explore new opportunities for income. Be mindful of impulsive spending—direct energy toward building stability instead. This is also a day to affirm your worth; when you value yourself, others do too. Leo, abundance is not just financial—it's the confidence to demand fairness and honor your talents.

Affirmation & Gratitude
"I honor my worth and manage my resources wisely, creating lasting abundance."

Leo
21 August 2026

The Moon moves into your communication zone, encouraging dialogue, writing, and learning. Conversations may feel especially important, bringing clarity or opportunity. Networking thrives, and your words carry influence. Avoid dominating discussions—listening is just as powerful as speaking. Leo, your storytelling captivates, but sincerity builds trust. Today is about using your voice not to command but to connect. A casual chat could become the spark that changes your direction.

Affirmation & Gratitude

"I communicate with clarity and sincerity, creating harmony and opportunity."

Leo
22 August 2026

The Sun enters Virgo, turning your focus toward finances, self-worth, and security for the next month. This cycle emphasizes building stability and aligning values with actions. Today, you may feel drawn to set financial goals or create a plan for abundance. Leo, your fiery ambition thrives when paired with grounded structure. Today marks the start of a season for practical growth—use it to create a secure foundation for your dreams.

Affirmation & Gratitude

"I align my values with action, creating security that empowers my dreams."

Leo
23 August 2026

The Moon highlights your home and family, urging you to focus on roots and stability. Domestic conversations may bring healing, or you may crave comfort in familiar spaces. Projects at home also flourish. Leo, while your pride often seeks external recognition, today is about the private spaces that sustain you. Nurturing family and creating peace at home will restore balance and give you strength to face the outside world.

Affirmation & Gratitude
"I nurture my home and family, honoring the roots of my strength."

Leo
24 August 2026

The Moon lights your joy and creativity sector, sparking inspiration, romance, and playfulness. You'll feel drawn to hobbies, art, or leisure that excites you. Romance feels vibrant, and creative breakthroughs may surface. Leo, joy is not frivolous—it's essential. By embracing play, you fuel the fire that carries you toward greater achievements. Today is about celebrating what makes you feel alive—your spark is contagious, and others are inspired by your glow.

Affirmation & Gratitude
"I embrace joy and creativity, letting passion fuel my fire."

Leo
25 August 2026

The Moon emphasizes health, routines, and productivity. You may feel motivated to refine daily habits, organize, or focus on wellness. This is an excellent day for tackling tasks and creating sustainable routines. Though structure may feel dull, it strengthens your vitality and supports bigger dreams. Leo, success is built on consistency. Today reminds you that small steps taken regularly create the foundation for your brightest ambitions to flourish.

Affirmation & Gratitude

"I strengthen myself with discipline and balance, honoring routines that empower my fire."

Leo
26 August 2026

The Moon moves into your partnership sector, shining a light on relationships. Romantic bonds may deepen, or professional collaborations could gain momentum. Compromise and cooperation are key—avoid letting pride block progress. Harmony is possible if you honor balance and empathy. Leo, true strength is found in connection, not control. Today is about building bridges, not walls. By sharing your light generously, you create love and loyalty that lasts.

Affirmation & Gratitude

"I honor love and cooperation, creating balance in my relationships."

Leo
27 August 2026

The Moon highlights your exploration and learning zone, sparking curiosity. You may crave new experiences—travel, study, or diving into fresh ideas. Even small acts like reading or engaging in deep conversations can broaden your perspective. Spiritually, breakthroughs are possible if you open yourself to new insights. Leo, your fire burns brighter when you stretch beyond routine. Today invites you to expand horizons and embrace growth that feeds both your heart and spirit.

Affirmation & Gratitude

"I welcome new horizons, letting curiosity expand my spirit."

Leo
28 August 2026

The Moon activates your career sector, drawing attention to ambition, recognition, and responsibility. You may be asked to step into leadership or showcase your talents. While your natural charisma shines, humility ensures long-lasting respect. Today is a powerful moment to push a project forward or claim recognition for your hard work. Leo, your roar inspires confidence, but reliability cements trust. Align passion with consistency to build your legacy.

Affirmation & Gratitude
"I step into leadership with humility and strength, proving my worth through action."

Leo
29 August 2026

A quieter energy arrives as the Moon enters your spiritual and inner world. You may crave solitude, rest, or reflection. Intuition is heightened, so pay attention to dreams and subtle nudges. This isn't a day for outward hustle—it's for recharging. Leo, your pride thrives in the spotlight, but true wisdom comes when you honor silence. Today's rest is not wasted—it prepares you for the fiery steps ahead. Trust the pause.

Affirmation & Gratitude

"I honor stillness, knowing reflection renews my fire."

Leo
30 August 2026

The Moon moves into your sign, amplifying vitality, confidence, and charisma. Energy rises, and you may feel ready to act boldly on personal goals. Others notice your glow easily—use this attention wisely. Romance, creativity, and leadership opportunities all thrive today. Leo, your natural magnetism draws admiration, but your true gift lies in inspiring others. Shine authentically and generously—your fire ignites confidence in everyone around you.

Affirmation & Gratitude

"I shine authentically, inspiring others with my light and generosity."

Leo
31 August 2026

The Moon emphasizes finances and self-worth, urging reflection on resources. You may feel motivated to budget, save, or pursue opportunities for income. Abundance grows when you align choices with gratitude and wisdom. Avoid impulsive spending—focus on stability and long-term security. Leo, true wealth comes not only from material gain but from valuing yourself deeply. Stand tall in your worth, and abundance will naturally flow toward you.

Affirmation & Gratitude

"I honor my worth and make choices that create lasting abundance."

September 2026

Leo
01 September 2026

The Moon highlights communication, making today ideal for important conversations, teaching, or networking. Your words hold influence—professionally, proposals thrive; personally, heartfelt talks bring healing. Be mindful of tone; balance strength with kindness. A casual chat could spark opportunity. Leo, your roar commands attention, but your thoughtful words inspire loyalty. Today is about using your voice to connect meaningfully and open new doors for growth.

Affirmation & Gratitude

"I communicate with clarity and warmth, building bridges of trust and opportunity."

Leo
02 September 2026

The Moon emphasizes home and family, reminding you to nurture your roots. Domestic projects, heartfelt conversations, or simply enjoying time at home bring peace. You may feel called to balance ambition with stability. Leo, though you shine in the outer world, your private foundation sustains you. Today, tend to those who love you unconditionally—their support strengthens your fire. A grounded home fuels your brightest success.

Affirmation & Gratitude
"I nurture my home and loved ones, honoring the roots of my strength."

Leo
03 September 2026

The Moon lights your creativity and romance zone, infusing the day with joy, passion, and inspiration. You'll feel playful and expressive, eager to dive into hobbies, art, or leisure that uplifts your spirit. Relationships also sparkle, with romance flowing more freely. Professionally, fresh ideas break through—don't dismiss sudden flashes of insight. Leo, joy is not indulgence; it's your power source. Today is about leaning into pleasure unapologetically and allowing joy to recharge your fire.

Affirmation & Gratitude

"I embrace joy and creativity, letting passion and play fuel my fire."

Leo
04 September 2026

The Moon emphasizes health, routines, and productivity. You may feel compelled to refine habits, clear clutter, or establish structure in your schedule. Wellness choices are powerful now—small steps in exercise, diet, or rest bring big results. Though you crave bold achievements, Leo, today is about building balance. Consistency supports your long-term ambitions. Discipline isn't about restriction—it's empowerment. Choose sustainable actions, and you'll feel stronger, freer, and more aligned with your purpose.

Affirmation & Gratitude
"I create balance through healthy habits, strengthening my body and spirit."

Leo
05 September 2026

Relationships come into focus as the Moon activates your partnership sector. Romantic bonds deepen through meaningful conversation or affection, while professional teamwork thrives. Compromise is essential—avoid letting pride hinder progress. Today is about cooperation, not competition. Leo, your warmth makes others feel valued, but true leadership means sharing the stage. By nurturing harmony, you create partnerships that uplift both you and those around you.

Affirmation & Gratitude

"I honor cooperation and love, creating harmony in all my relationships."

Leo
06 September 2026

The Moon moves into your exploration zone, stirring curiosity and adventure. You may feel restless for travel, study, or spiritual discovery. Even small acts—reading, journaling, or exploring new ideas—expand your horizons. Inspiration flows when you stretch beyond the ordinary. Leo, your fire grows brighter when you feed it with knowledge and experience. Today's cosmic nudge asks you to embrace discovery—it will spark wisdom and renew your courage.

Affirmation & Gratitude

"I embrace new horizons, letting curiosity guide my growth."

Leo
07 September 2026

The Moon highlights your career sector, bringing visibility and ambition. You may receive recognition for past efforts or feel inspired to pursue a leadership role. This is a day to showcase your reliability alongside your charisma. Balance pride with humility—respect grows through both. Leo, today is about proving that your roar is backed by substance. Take a bold but practical step forward—this moment plants seeds for lasting success.

Affirmation & Gratitude

"I step into leadership with confidence and humility, building my legacy."

Leo
08 September 2026

A quieter tone flows as the Moon enters your spiritual and inner world. You may crave solitude, meditation, or reflection. Intuition is heightened, and guidance may arrive through dreams or synchronicities. Don't resist this inward pull—today is for restoration, not outward striving. Leo, honoring stillness doesn't dim your fire; it refuels it. This pause helps you prepare for bolder moves ahead. Trust that your inner wisdom carries the answers you seek.

Affirmation & Gratitude

"I honor stillness and intuition, trusting reflection renews my spirit."

Leo
09 September 2026

The Moon moves into your sign, amplifying charisma, vitality, and confidence. You'll feel magnetic, ready to pursue goals or showcase talents. Others notice your presence easily—use this attention wisely. Romance and creativity thrive, while leadership opportunities arise. Leo, this is your day to shine unapologetically. Remember: true strength uplifts others as much as it celebrates itself. Share your light generously, and you'll inspire admiration and loyalty.

Affirmation & Gratitude

"I shine authentically, inspiring others with my warmth and generosity."

Leo
10 September 2026

The Moon emphasizes finances and self-worth, pulling focus to how you manage resources and value yourself. You may feel motivated to budget, negotiate, or plan for long-term stability. Avoid impulsive purchases—choose wisely, and abundance will follow. Leo, true wealth is not just money; it's self-respect. When you honor your worth, opportunities naturally align. Today is about affirming your value through practical actions that support both security and freedom.

Affirmation & Gratitude

"I honor my worth and make wise choices that attract abundance."

Leo
11 September 2026

The Moon lights your communication zone, favoring conversations, writing, and networking. Your words carry influence today—professionally, you may impress with presentations; personally, heartfelt talks heal misunderstandings. Be mindful of tone—balance confidence with compassion. Leo, your roar is powerful, but it's your thoughtful voice that builds bridges. A casual chat could bring surprising opportunity. Today is about using communication as your most magnetic tool for connection and progress.

Affirmation & Gratitude

"I use my words with clarity and warmth, creating trust and opportunity."

Leo
12 September 2026

The Moon highlights home and family, drawing attention to your private world. Domestic projects, repairs, or quality time with loved ones may call. Though your pride often seeks the spotlight, today is about grounding. Emotional conversations with family could bring peace or closure. Leo, your roar is sustained by strong roots. By nurturing those who love you unconditionally, you fuel the fire that powers your ambitions.

Affirmation & Gratitude

"I nurture my home and family, honoring the roots that sustain me."

Leo
13 September 2026

The Moon moves into your creativity and romance sector, igniting inspiration and joy. You may feel drawn to hobbies, art, or playful connections. Romantic energy is strong, and sparks may surprise you. Professionally, creative ideas bring breakthroughs—don't dismiss unusual insights. Leo, joy is your natural magnetism—it replenishes your energy and attracts admiration. Today is about celebrating life's pleasures and letting your light shine through fun and self-expression.

Affirmation & Gratitude

"I embrace joy and creativity, letting passion fuel my fire."

Leo
14 September 2026

The Moon emphasizes health, wellness, and routines, encouraging productivity. You may feel driven to refine habits, reorganize, or address tasks left undone. Though mundane, these steps empower long-term ambitions. Leo, discipline may feel restrictive, but it actually gives freedom—it sustains your fire when energy wanes. By focusing on consistency, you create stability that fuels greater achievements. Today is about honoring your body and environment as allies in success.

Affirmation & Gratitude

"I strengthen my routines with discipline, fueling my vitality and freedom."

Leo
15 September 2026

Relationships take priority as the Moon enters your partnership zone. Romantic bonds deepen, or professional collaborations bring progress. Compromise and empathy are essential—avoid letting pride block harmony. Leo, your charisma draws people in, but real strength lies in cooperation. Today is about sharing your light generously and valuing balance. When you honor connection, relationships flourish, and loyalty grows stronger.

Affirmation & Gratitude

"I honor love and cooperation, creating harmony in all my relationships."

Leo
16 September 2026

A Lunar Eclipse in Pisces illuminates your intimacy and transformation sector. Emotional revelations about shared resources, trust, or vulnerability may surface. You may be asked to release old patterns or fears, making space for renewal. Though intense, this eclipse brings healing if you face truths honestly. Leo, courage is your gift—use it now to step into transformation. Today marks a turning point in how you share and connect deeply.

Affirmation & Gratitude
"I embrace transformation with courage, releasing the old to welcome renewal."

Leo
17 September 2026

The Moon shifts into your exploration and higher learning zone, lifting the heaviness of yesterday's eclipse. You may crave travel, study, or spiritual practices that expand your perspective. Curiosity sparks inspiration, and even small steps toward new knowledge refresh your spirit. Conversations with diverse people bring wisdom. Leo, growth happens when you stretch beyond familiar ground. Today is about seeking adventure—physical, mental, or spiritual—that reignites your inner fire and opens your path.

Affirmation & Gratitude

"I welcome new horizons, letting curiosity and growth expand my fire."

Leo
18 September 2026

The Moon activates your career and ambition sector, spotlighting goals, recognition, and responsibility. You may be asked to lead or to prove your reliability in a key project. Recognition flows naturally if you balance charisma with humility. Leo, your roar inspires, but substance cements respect. Today is about aligning actions with ambition to build a foundation of trust and legacy. A bold step forward now shapes long-term success.

Affirmation & Gratitude

"I step confidently into leadership, proving my strength through dedication."

Leo
19 September 2026

A quieter rhythm emerges as the Moon enters your spiritual and inner world. Intuition is heightened, and dreams may reveal guidance. You may feel pulled to withdraw from busyness to recharge. Leo, you thrive in the spotlight, but your power also grows in stillness. Today, rest is not retreat—it's preparation. By listening inwardly, you fuel your courage to shine outwardly tomorrow. Honor this pause; it restores your fire.

Affirmation & Gratitude
"I honor stillness and intuition, trusting reflection renews my strength."

Leo
20 September 2026

The Moon enters your sign, boosting vitality, confidence, and visibility. You'll feel magnetic and eager to pursue goals, romance, or creative projects. This is your day to roar unapologetically—yet remember, true leadership uplifts others too. Leo, shine authentically and generously. Your presence naturally inspires those around you. Today is about celebrating yourself and using your energy to light the way for others as well.

Affirmation & Gratitude
"I shine authentically, inspiring others with my light and generosity."

Leo

21 September 2026

The Moon emphasizes finances and self-worth, drawing your attention to security and values. You may feel driven to budget, negotiate, or reassess your relationship with money. Avoid impulsive spending; instead, focus on wise, long-term stability. Leo, true wealth comes when you respect yourself enough to make choices that honor your value. Today is about aligning confidence with practicality—when you stand tall in your worth, abundance naturally follows.

Affirmation & Gratitude

"I honor my worth, making wise choices that create abundance."

Leo
22 September 2026

The Moon activates communication, favoring important conversations, networking, and learning. Your words carry weight and charisma today, so speak with clarity and sincerity. A discussion could open doors, heal misunderstandings, or bring opportunity. Leo, your roar is commanding, but your thoughtful voice creates deeper trust. Balance speaking with listening to amplify your influence. Today is about sharing your truth in ways that inspire loyalty and connection.

Affirmation & Gratitude

"I communicate with clarity and warmth, creating harmony and opportunity."

Leo
23 September 2026

The Sun enters Libra, spotlighting your communication and networking zone for the month ahead. This cycle emphasizes relationships, writing, teaching, and sharing ideas. Today, you may feel inspired to connect with friends, colleagues, or communities. Leo, your natural magnetism grows when you use it to bridge connections. This is a time to let your voice shine and to welcome collaborations. Your words can shape influence and opportunity now.

Affirmation & Gratitude

"I use my voice to inspire, connect, and create opportunities."

Leo
24 September 2026

The Moon highlights home and family, encouraging you to focus on roots, comfort, and stability. Domestic matters may need attention, or you may simply crave peace in your space. Conversations with loved ones bring healing, while tending to your environment restores balance. Leo, though you thrive in the outside world, your private sanctuary fuels your fire. Today is about nurturing the people and spaces that support you unconditionally. Strong roots empower your greatest achievements.

Affirmation & Gratitude

"I nurture my home and loved ones, honoring the foundation of my strength."

Leo

25 September 2026

The Moon lights up your creative and romantic zone, sparking joy, self-expression, and playfulness. You may feel inspired to pursue art, hobbies, or simply indulge in fun. Romance is heightened—single or partnered, your magnetism shines. Professionally, innovative ideas flow, offering breakthroughs if you follow inspiration. Leo, joy is your superpower—when you embrace it, opportunities multiply. Today is about celebrating what lights you up and sharing that radiance with others.

Affirmation & Gratitude

"I embrace joy and creativity, letting passion fuel my fire."

Leo
26 September 2026

The Moon emphasizes health, routines, and productivity, urging you to refine habits or tackle unfinished tasks. You may feel motivated to focus on exercise, diet, or organization. Though not glamorous, these efforts strengthen your vitality and free you for bigger dreams. Leo, discipline isn't restriction—it's empowerment. Today is about honoring your body and daily life as sacred. By making small, consistent improvements, you ensure your fire burns brighter and longer.

Affirmation & Gratitude

"I strengthen my routines with balance and discipline, sustaining my fire."

Leo
27 September 2026

Relationships take center stage as the Moon enters your partnership zone. Harmony flows more easily, making it a good day for romance, collaboration, or teamwork. If tensions linger, this is the perfect moment to resolve them with honesty and empathy. Leo, your pride sometimes resists compromise, but cooperation multiplies success. Today is about valuing connection as much as independence—when you share your light, it magnifies in return.

Affirmation & Gratitude

"I honor love and cooperation, creating harmony in my relationships."

Leo

28 September 2026

The Moon moves into your exploration zone, igniting curiosity and adventure. You may feel inspired to study, travel, or dive into new ideas. Spiritually, breakthroughs are possible if you stay open. Today is about saying yes to growth, even in small steps. Leo, your fire thrives when fed with knowledge and inspiration. Trust curiosity—it's your guide to wisdom and freedom. Life expands when you do.

Affirmation & Gratitude

"I embrace curiosity and growth, letting new horizons expand my spirit."

Leo

29 September 2026

A Full Moon in Aries lights your expansion zone, magnifying themes of growth, travel, and learning. This lunation may bring a breakthrough in education, a spiritual awakening, or clarity about your bigger path. You're being asked to step boldly into new horizons. Leo, eclipses and full moons remind you: courage is your gift. Today is about claiming your freedom to explore and grow beyond limits. Say yes to adventure.

Affirmation & Gratitude

"I embrace expansion and courage, stepping boldly into new horizons."

Leo
30 September 2026

The Moon activates your career and ambition sector, bringing visibility and recognition. You may feel compelled to push projects forward or step into leadership. Recognition from superiors or colleagues is possible. Balance confidence with humility—true success is sustained when rooted in respect. Leo, your roar inspires, but your reliability secures trust. Today is about proving your strength through steady action as much as charisma. Shine in ways that last.

Affirmation & Gratitude
"I step into leadership with confidence and humility, building respect through action."

October
2026

Leo
01 October 2026

The Moon draws you inward, highlighting rest, reflection, and intuition. You may feel less social and more in need of solitude. Dreams and synchronicities carry guidance—don't dismiss subtle signs. This is a day to retreat, recharge, and honor your inner world. Leo, your pride often thrives in activity, but balance comes from stillness. Today isn't about external action—it's about preparing your fire for the next surge of growth.

Affirmation & Gratitude

"I honor stillness and intuition, trusting quiet moments renew my fire."

Leo
02 October 2026

The Moon enters your sign, boosting confidence, visibility, and magnetism. You'll feel vibrant and ready to take bold steps in love, career, or creativity. Others notice you easily—use this spotlight to inspire, not to dominate. Leo, authenticity is your most powerful gift. Today is about owning who you are unapologetically while sharing generosity and warmth. Shine brightly, but remember to lift others with you.

Affirmation & Gratitude
"I shine authentically, inspiring others with my warmth and confidence."

Leo
03 October 2026

The Moon highlights finances and self-worth, urging you to reflect on resources. You may feel motivated to review spending, budget, or seek fair compensation for your work. Avoid overspending on fleeting desires; instead, choose stability. Leo, abundance starts with honoring your value. When you respect yourself, others do the same. Today is about aligning money choices with long-term security and self-respect.

Affirmation & Gratitude
"I honor my worth, making wise choices that build lasting abundance."

Leo
04 October 2026

The Moon lights your communication zone, favoring conversations, writing, and learning. Words flow easily, making this a great day for meetings, proposals, or personal discussions. A casual chat may open unexpected doors. Be mindful of tone —balance strength with kindness. Leo, your roar commands attention, but your thoughtful voice builds trust. Today is about speaking from the heart and listening deeply.

Affirmation & Gratitude
"I communicate with clarity and warmth, building bridges of trust and opportunity."

Leo
05 October 2026

Home and family take center stage as the Moon shifts focus inward. Domestic responsibilities, projects, or quality time with loved ones feel important. This isn't a distraction—it's grounding. Leo, though your pride craves recognition in the outer world, your private life sustains you. Today is about strengthening your roots, creating peace at home, and appreciating those who support you unconditionally.

Affirmation & Gratitude

"I nurture my home and family, honoring the roots that sustain me."

Leo
06 October 2026

The Moon moves into your creative and romantic sector, sparking inspiration and joy. You may feel drawn to art, hobbies, or simply playful leisure. Romance is strong, and your charisma shines. Professionally, creative breakthroughs may appear—don't dismiss unusual insights. Leo, joy is not indulgence—it's a necessity. Today is about embracing fun and passion as tools that restore your brilliance and attract opportunities naturally.

Affirmation & Gratitude

"I embrace joy and creativity, letting passion fuel my spirit."

Leo
07 October 2026

The Moon emphasizes health, wellness, and routines. Productivity feels easier, and you'll want to refine habits, organize, or tackle lingering tasks. Wellness choices matter more now—small steps can have big impact. Leo, while your pride thrives on big achievements, discipline is the key to sustaining them. Today is about honoring your body and creating consistency that supports long-term vitality. Success is built daily.

Affirmation & Gratitude
"I strengthen myself through balance and healthy routines, fueling my long-term fire."

Leo
08 October 2026

The Moon highlights your partnership sector, bringing relationships—romantic and professional—into focus. Compromise and cooperation are essential today. If partnered, nurture affection with empathy; if single, connections may spark unexpectedly. Professionally, teamwork thrives, but avoid pride-driven conflicts. Leo, your charisma attracts loyalty, but real strength lies in balance and fairness. Today is about sharing your light with others and recognizing the beauty of mutual growth. Harmony now strengthens bonds for the future.

Affirmation & Gratitude

"I honor cooperation and love, creating harmony in my relationships."

Leo
09 October 2026

The Moon moves into your exploration sector, sparking curiosity, inspiration, and adventure. You may crave travel, learning, or fresh perspectives. Even small actions—reading, journaling, or speaking with diverse people—broaden your horizons. Spiritually, breakthroughs may arrive if you stay open. Leo, your fire thrives when fueled by discovery. Today is about stepping beyond comfort zones and embracing growth with courage and excitement.

Affirmation & Gratitude

"I welcome new horizons, letting curiosity guide my growth."

Leo
10 October 2026

The Moon activates your career zone, bringing visibility, recognition, and ambition. You may be called to lead, present, or prove your reliability. Recognition is possible if you balance pride with humility. Leo, your roar inspires others, but true leadership is earned through consistency and action. Today, take a bold yet grounded step toward long-term success. Your legacy grows stronger when your charisma is matched by responsibility.

Affirmation & Gratitude
"I step into leadership with confidence and humility, building lasting respect."

Leo
11 October 2026

A quieter rhythm emerges as the Moon enters your spiritual and inner world. You may feel pulled to retreat, meditate, or reflect. Intuition is heightened—listen closely to dreams and inner nudges. Though your pride enjoys action, today's power lies in stillness. Leo, honoring your inner fire ensures your outer shine lasts. Rest is not weakness—it's wisdom. By recharging, you prepare for your next bold move.

Affirmation & Gratitude

"I honor stillness and intuition, trusting rest renews my fire."

Leo
12 October 2026

The Moon enters your sign, amplifying confidence, charisma, and vitality. You'll feel magnetic, eager to pursue goals, romance, or creative projects. Others notice your presence easily—use it to inspire rather than overshadow. Leo, today is about celebrating your authentic self while also uplifting others. Your natural glow is irresistible, but your generosity makes it unforgettable. Shine boldly, but share the spotlight too—it magnifies your influence.

Affirmation & Gratitude
"I shine authentically, inspiring others with my light and generosity."

Leo
13 October 2026

The Moon emphasizes finances and self-worth, encouraging you to reflect on resources and values. You may feel inspired to budget, save, or request recognition for your contributions. Avoid impulsive spending—long-term stability is your focus. Leo, abundance flows when you honor your worth and align choices with gratitude. Today is about affirming your value through practical actions that create security and empowerment for the future.

Affirmation & Gratitude
"I honor my worth, making wise choices that attract abundance."

Leo
14 October 2026

The Moon highlights communication, making this a powerful day for speaking, writing, and connecting. Conversations may bring clarity, healing, or opportunity. Networking thrives, and your words inspire others easily. Be mindful of tone—balance strength with kindness. Leo, your roar commands attention, but your thoughtful words build trust and loyalty. Today is about using your voice as a bridge for understanding and progress. Speak with sincerity, and doors will open.

Affirmation & Gratitude

"I communicate with clarity and warmth, creating harmony and opportunity."

Leo
15 October 2026

The Moon emphasizes home and family, encouraging you to focus on roots and stability. Domestic matters may need attention, or you may crave quiet time with loved ones. Simple acts—sharing meals, cleaning, or heartfelt talks—bring grounding and peace. Leo, though your pride often craves recognition, your strength also lies in nurturing the foundation that sustains you. Today is about tending to your private world so your outer roar grows stronger.

Affirmation & Gratitude

"I nurture my home and loved ones, honoring the roots that sustain me."

Leo
16 October 2026

The Moon moves into your creativity and romance sector, sparking playfulness, joy, and inspiration. Hobbies, art, and leisure bring fulfillment, while romantic connections feel vibrant and exciting. Professionally, creative breakthroughs are possible—follow sparks of inspiration. Leo, joy is not frivolous—it's your natural state, the source of your magnetism. Today is about celebrating life unapologetically, allowing play to fuel your spirit and attract admiration naturally.

Affirmation & Gratitude

"I embrace joy and creativity, letting passion inspire my brilliance."

Leo
17 October 2026

The Moon highlights health, routines, and productivity, urging you to refine habits and address unfinished tasks. Wellness and organization are emphasized, giving you energy to move forward. Though routines may feel dull, they provide the discipline needed for greater achievements. Leo, consistency is your ally—it ensures your fire doesn't burn out too quickly. Today's small improvements build long-term vitality and freedom. Treat discipline as empowerment, not limitation.

Affirmation & Gratitude

"I strengthen my routines with balance and discipline, sustaining my fire."

Leo
18 October 2026

Relationships come into focus as the Moon enters your partnership zone. Romance deepens through affection and honesty, while professional teamwork flows more smoothly. Compromise and empathy are essential—avoid letting pride dominate. Leo, true strength lies in cooperation. Today is about balancing independence with connection, valuing others as much as yourself. By sharing your warmth generously, you create bonds built on loyalty and mutual respect.

Affirmation & Gratitude

"I honor cooperation and love, creating harmony in my relationships."

Leo
19 October 2026

The Moon moves into your exploration and higher learning zone, awakening curiosity. You may feel inspired to travel, study, or expand your spiritual practices. Even small actions—journaling, reading, or embracing new perspectives—spark growth. Leo, your fire thrives when fed with discovery. Today is about seeking inspiration in unfamiliar places, allowing adventure to ignite wisdom. Open your mind, and new opportunities will follow.

Affirmation & Gratitude

"I embrace new horizons, letting curiosity expand my fire."

Leo
20 October 2026

The Moon activates your career sector, drawing attention to ambition and recognition. You may be asked to step into leadership or feel inspired to push projects forward. Recognition is likely if you balance confidence with humility. Leo, your roar is magnetic, but it's consistency that builds trust. Today is about proving your strength through reliable action as well as charm. Take one bold step toward long-term goals now.

Affirmation & Gratitude

"I step confidently into leadership, proving my strength through dedication."

Leo
21 October 2026

The Moon enters your spiritual and inner world, encouraging rest and reflection. Intuition is heightened—dreams and synchronicities may offer guidance. Avoid pushing too hard; today is about recharging and honoring your inner fire. Leo, you thrive in the spotlight, but wisdom comes from stillness. Quiet moments renew your courage to roar more powerfully later. Trust that today's pause is fuel for tomorrow's brilliance.

Affirmation & Gratitude

"I honor stillness and intuition, trusting reflection restores my strength."

Leo

22 October 2026

The Moon enters your sign, boosting charisma, confidence, and vitality. You'll feel ready to pursue goals, romance, or creative projects with boldness. Others notice your energy easily—this is your moment to shine. Just remember: true leadership uplifts others rather than overshadowing them. Leo, today is about celebrating your authentic self unapologetically while inspiring those around you with warmth. Your roar is powerful, but your generosity makes it unforgettable.

Affirmation & Gratitude

"I shine authentically, inspiring others with my warmth and confidence."

Leo
23 October 2026

The Moon emphasizes finances and self-worth, urging you to review your relationship with money and value. You may feel compelled to budget, save, or ask for recognition. Avoid impulsive spending—focus on building security. Leo, abundance flows when paired with gratitude and wise decisions. Today is about affirming your worth through practical choices that strengthen your future. Stand tall in your value, and opportunities for prosperity will follow.

Affirmation & Gratitude

"I honor my worth, making wise choices that attract abundance."

Leo
24 October 2026

The Moon highlights communication, making today ideal for conversations, networking, and learning. Your words carry weight and magnetism, so use them carefully. Professionally, this is an excellent day for presentations or proposals; personally, heartfelt talks bring healing. Leo, your roar commands attention, but your thoughtful voice builds trust. Today is about balancing confidence with compassion in communication, allowing you to influence and inspire meaningfully.

Affirmation & Gratitude

"I use my words with clarity and warmth, creating harmony and opportunity."

Leo
25 October 2026

The Moon shifts into your home and family zone, encouraging you to focus on your private world. Domestic projects, family conversations, or simply creating comfort restore balance. Though your pride loves the spotlight, roots sustain your fire. Leo, today is about cherishing the foundation that supports you. By nurturing loved ones and tending to your environment, you create stability that fuels greater ambitions in the outside world.

Affirmation & Gratitude

"I nurture my home and loved ones, honoring the roots that sustain me."

Leo
26 October 2026

The Moon energizes your creativity and romance sector, filling the day with joy, passion, and playfulness. Hobbies and art flourish, while romantic sparks feel stronger. Professionally, creative ideas break through routine—don't dismiss inspiration. Leo, joy is your natural magnetism. When you embrace fun and passion, opportunities appear effortlessly. Today is about letting your heart lead and celebrating what makes you feel alive.

Affirmation & Gratitude

"I embrace joy and creativity, letting passion fuel my fire."

Leo
27 October 2026

The Moon highlights health, wellness, and routines, urging you to refine daily habits. You may feel driven to exercise, declutter, or bring order to tasks. Though routines seem small, they build strength and vitality that support greater ambitions. Leo, discipline doesn't dim your fire—it sustains it. Today, focus on small steps that align your body, mind, and spirit with long-term goals.

Affirmation & Gratitude

"I strengthen myself with balance and healthy routines, sustaining my fire."

Leo
28 October 2026

Relationships take center stage as the Moon enters your partnership sector. Harmony flows more easily, making this an ideal day for romance or teamwork. If tensions linger, honest and empathetic conversations can restore peace. Leo, your pride sometimes resists compromise, but today proves cooperation creates deeper trust. Shared success always feels sweeter. By valuing balance, you create loyalty and bonds that last.

Affirmation & Gratitude

"I honor love and cooperation, creating balance in my relationships."

Leo
29 October 2026

The Moon shifts into your exploration zone, sparking curiosity and inspiration. You may crave new experiences—travel, learning, or spiritual growth. Even simple steps like reading or trying a fresh routine broaden your horizons. Conversations with diverse people can bring wisdom and expand perspective. Leo, your fire thrives when you reach beyond the familiar. Today is about saying yes to discovery and letting your adventurous side guide you toward growth.

Affirmation & Gratitude

"I embrace curiosity and growth, letting new horizons expand my fire."

Leo
30 October 2026

The Moon activates your career and ambition sector, bringing visibility and recognition. A project may peak, or a leadership opportunity arises. You're noticed more easily today—step confidently into the spotlight, but temper confidence with humility. Leo, your roar is inspiring, but respect comes from reliability. Today is about aligning charisma with substance to prove you're more than charm—you're consistent and dependable too.

Affirmation & Gratitude

"I step into leadership with humility and strength, building trust through action."

Leo
31 October 2026

A quieter rhythm flows as the Moon enters your spiritual and inner world. You may crave solitude, meditation, or journaling. Intuition is heightened, offering subtle guidance—don't ignore dreams or inner nudges. Though your pride thrives in activity, today's lesson is that wisdom comes through stillness. Leo, by honoring your inner fire, you prepare for the external spotlight. Rest is not retreat—it's renewal. Trust the pause as sacred.

Affirmation & Gratitude

"I honor stillness and intuition, knowing reflection renews my spirit."

November 2026

Leo
01 November 2026

The Moon moves into your sign, amplifying vitality, charisma, and visibility. You'll feel more confident and ready to act boldly in love, career, or creativity. Opportunities to showcase talents or take leadership flow easily. Be mindful of ego—your influence is strongest when paired with generosity. Leo, today is your day to shine authentically and celebrate yourself while inspiring others with your warmth and courage.

Affirmation & Gratitude

"I shine authentically, inspiring others with my light and generosity."

Leo

02 November 2026

The Moon emphasizes finances and self-worth, drawing your attention to money and value. You may feel motivated to budget, request recognition, or explore new income opportunities. Avoid impulsive spending—abundance grows when you align choices with wisdom and gratitude. Leo, prosperity isn't only about resources; it's about how you honor yourself. Today is about standing tall in your value and acting in alignment with it.

Affirmation & Gratitude

"I honor my worth and make wise choices that build abundance."

Leo
03 November 2026

The Moon activates your communication zone, making it an excellent day for writing, speaking, or networking. Your words carry influence and magnetism, so use them carefully. A conversation may bring healing or opportunity. Be mindful to balance speaking with listening—insight comes from both. Leo, your roar can command attention, but your thoughtful words inspire lasting loyalty. Today is about connecting meaningfully through language.

Affirmation & Gratitude

"I use my voice with clarity and warmth, creating trust and opportunity."

Leo
04 November 2026

The Moon highlights home and family, drawing focus to your roots. Domestic projects or conversations may bring healing and grounding. You may crave comfort in familiar spaces. Though your pride seeks recognition, your true power is sustained by a stable foundation. Leo, today is about nurturing those who love you unconditionally and creating peace in your personal space. Strong roots ensure your fire burns brighter in the outside world.

Affirmation & Gratitude

"I nurture my home and loved ones, honoring the roots of my strength."

Leo
05 November 2026

The Moon moves into your creativity and romance sector, sparking joy, playfulness, and inspiration. Hobbies and art call your attention, while romance feels especially vibrant. Professionally, fresh ideas may bring breakthroughs—follow sparks of inspiration without hesitation. Leo, joy isn't indulgence—it's your natural fuel. When you embrace passion and play, opportunities multiply. Today is about leaning into what excites you, letting fun and creativity energize your spirit.

Affirmation & Gratitude

"I embrace joy and creativity, letting passion fuel my fire."

Leo
06 November 2026

The Moon emphasizes health, routines, and productivity, urging you to refine habits. You may feel motivated to exercise, reorganize, or tackle long-delayed tasks. Though routine may seem tedious, consistency builds freedom. Leo, your fire burns brightest when supported by balance. Today, small, sustainable steps matter more than dramatic action. Treat your body and environment as allies in your success—they sustain the brilliance you share with the world.

Affirmation & Gratitude
"I strengthen myself with balance and healthy routines, fueling my long-term fire."

Leo

07 November 2026

The Moon highlights relationships, drawing attention to partnerships in love and work. Harmony flows easily if you value cooperation and balance. Romantic connections deepen through kindness and honesty, while professional collaborations thrive with mutual respect. Avoid letting pride dominate—true leadership uplifts. Leo, today is about remembering that strength is not diminished by compromise but enriched by connection. Share your light generously, and bonds will strengthen.

Affirmation & Gratitude

"I honor cooperation and love, creating harmony in my relationships."

Leo

08 November 2026

The Moon enters your exploration sector, stirring curiosity and a desire for adventure. You may crave travel, learning, or new experiences. Even small actions—reading, journaling, or meeting someone new—expand your perspective. Spiritually, breakthroughs are possible if you stay open. Leo, your fire grows when you feed it discovery. Today is about saying yes to exploration, embracing growth that refreshes your heart and sharpens your vision.

Affirmation & Gratitude

"I embrace curiosity and growth, letting new horizons expand my fire."

Leo

09 November 2026

The Moon activates your career and ambition sector, spotlighting recognition and responsibility. You may be called to lead, present, or finalize an important project. Recognition flows naturally when charisma is matched with consistency. Leo, your roar inspires confidence, but your reliability earns respect. Today is about proving your strength through action, aligning ambition with integrity. Step forward with confidence—opportunities now can shape your long-term legacy.

Affirmation & Gratitude

"I step confidently into leadership, proving my strength through action."

Leo
10 November 2026

A quieter rhythm unfolds as the Moon moves into your spiritual and inner world. You may feel called to rest, reflect, or retreat. Intuition is strong—pay attention to dreams or synchronicities. Though you prefer the spotlight, Leo, your greatest insights sometimes emerge in solitude. Today's pause restores energy and strengthens your inner fire, preparing you for tomorrow's bold steps. Honor reflection as part of your power.

Affirmation & Gratitude

"I honor stillness and intuition, trusting reflection renews my spirit."

Leo

11 November 2026

The Moon enters your sign, amplifying confidence, vitality, and charisma. You'll feel magnetic and ready to take bold action in love, creativity, or leadership. Others notice you easily—use this visibility to inspire, not dominate. Leo, today is about celebrating your authentic self and reminding others that leadership uplifts. Shine unapologetically, but with warmth. When you share your fire generously, admiration and loyalty naturally follow.

Affirmation & Gratitude

"I shine authentically, inspiring others with my light and generosity."

Leo

12 November 2026

The Moon emphasizes finances and self-worth, encouraging you to reflect on resources, income, and security. You may feel motivated to budget, renegotiate, or invest wisely. Avoid impulsive purchases—choose stability and value over temporary indulgence. Leo, abundance flows when you align your choices with gratitude and respect for your worth. Today is about standing tall in your value and ensuring your financial foundation matches your ambition. Self-respect attracts prosperity naturally.

Affirmation & Gratitude

"I honor my worth and make wise choices that build lasting abundance."

Leo
13 November 2026

The Moon highlights communication, favoring conversations, writing, and learning. Your words carry extra weight today—professionally, pitches and presentations succeed; personally, heartfelt talks heal or inspire. Networking flows easily, but remember to balance speaking with listening. Leo, your roar is powerful, but your thoughtful voice builds trust and loyalty. Today is about using language to connect meaningfully and plant seeds for future opportunities.

Affirmation & Gratitude

"I use my words with clarity and warmth, creating trust and opportunity."

Leo
14 November 2026

The Moon moves into your home and family zone, pulling your attention inward. Domestic projects, family conversations, or simple nurturing acts create harmony. Though your pride thrives in the spotlight, your private world sustains your fire. Today is about cherishing the people and places that give you strength. Leo, when you care for your roots, your roar grows stronger in the world. Create balance between ambition and home life.

Affirmation & Gratitude

"I nurture my home and family, honoring the roots that sustain me."

Leo
15 November 2026

The Moon energizes your creative and romantic sector, filling the day with joy, passion, and inspiration. You may feel drawn to hobbies, art, or leisure that restores your fire. Romance may sparkle with affection and fun. Professionally, creative breakthroughs flow easily—follow sudden sparks. Leo, joy is not indulgence—it's your natural magnetism. Today is about celebrating what lights you up and sharing that brilliance generously.

Affirmation & Gratitude

"I embrace joy and creativity, letting passion fuel my spirit."

Leo
16 November 2026

The Moon emphasizes health, wellness, and productivity, urging you to refine routines. You may feel compelled to organize, exercise, or clear clutter. Though it may feel mundane, these choices sustain your vitality. Leo, consistency is what keeps your fire burning strong over time. Today is about treating small habits as sacred acts of self-respect. When your body and mind are balanced, your spirit soars.

Affirmation & Gratitude

"I strengthen my routines with balance and discipline, sustaining my fire."

Leo
17 November 2026

The Moon lights up your partnership sector, putting relationships in focus. Romantic connections deepen through empathy, while professional collaborations thrive through balance and teamwork. Avoid letting pride dominate—compromise creates harmony. Leo, true strength is not diminished by cooperation; it is enhanced. Today, your warmth makes others feel valued, strengthening bonds of loyalty. Share your light generously—it shines brighter when reflected through connection.

Affirmation & Gratitude

"I honor love and cooperation, creating balance in my relationships."

Leo
18 November 2026

The Moon enters your exploration zone, sparking curiosity and adventure. You may crave travel, higher learning, or spiritual practices that expand your perspective. Even small steps—reading, journaling, or engaging with diverse people—bring growth. Leo, your fire thrives when you push beyond comfort zones. Today is about embracing the unknown and trusting that new horizons lead to wisdom and renewal.

Affirmation & Gratitude
"I embrace curiosity and growth, letting new horizons expand my spirit."

Leo
19 November 2026

The Moon activates your career and ambition zone, placing you in the spotlight. Recognition may arrive, or responsibilities increase, demanding your leadership. Step forward with confidence, but temper pride with humility. Leo, your roar inspires, but consistency cements respect. This is a day to show substance as well as charm. Align your energy with long-term goals—today's actions plant seeds for your legacy. Recognition and trust will grow from your reliability.

Affirmation & Gratitude

"I step into leadership with confidence and humility, proving my strength through action."

Leo
20 November 2026

The Moon shifts into your spiritual sector, slowing the pace and encouraging rest. You may feel drawn to solitude, meditation, or journaling. Intuition is heightened—pay attention to dreams or synchronicities. Though you thrive in action, Leo, today is about listening inwardly. Wisdom comes when you honor silence. Rest isn't retreat; it's renewal. Use this quiet energy to restore balance and prepare for your next bold step.

Affirmation & Gratitude

"I honor stillness and intuition, trusting reflection restores my fire."

Leo
21 November 2026

The Moon moves into your sign, amplifying confidence, vitality, and magnetism. Energy flows more easily, making this a great day for personal goals, romance, or creativity. Others notice your presence—use it to inspire, not overshadow. Leo, today is about celebrating your authentic self while remembering that true leadership uplifts others. Shine unapologetically, but with warmth. Your light is irresistible when shared generously.

Affirmation & Gratitude

"I shine authentically, inspiring others with my warmth and courage."

Leo
22 November 2026

The Moon emphasizes finances and self-worth, drawing attention to money matters and personal value. You may feel motivated to budget, negotiate, or plan for security. Avoid impulsive decisions; choose stability and gratitude instead. Leo, abundance grows when you honor yourself. Today is about affirming your worth through wise actions that support long-term prosperity. When you stand tall in your value, others reflect it back to you.

Affirmation & Gratitude

"I honor my worth, making wise choices that attract lasting abundance."

Leo

23 November 2026

The Moon highlights communication, making this a powerful day for dialogue, networking, and learning. Words flow easily, so use them with sincerity and warmth. Conversations can open doors, heal relationships, or inspire opportunity. Leo, your roar may command attention, but it's your thoughtful voice that earns loyalty. Today is about using language to build bridges and create progress. Speak from the heart, and your influence will ripple outward.

Affirmation & Gratitude

"I use my words with clarity and kindness, creating harmony and opportunity."

Leo
24 November 2026

The Moon enters your home and family zone, reminding you to nurture your foundation. Domestic matters may require attention, or you may crave quiet time in your sanctuary. Loved ones bring comfort, and emotional conversations may heal old wounds. Leo, your pride thrives in the outside world, but your fire depends on stability at home. Today is about creating peace in your private world to sustain your outer roar.

Affirmation & Gratitude
"I nurture my home and loved ones, honoring the roots that sustain me."

Leo

25 November 2026

The Moon energizes your creative and romantic sector, sparking inspiration and playfulness. You may feel drawn to art, hobbies, or leisure that uplifts your spirit. Romance also flourishes under this influence. Professionally, creative ideas break through—follow sparks of inspiration. Leo, joy isn't optional—it's essential to your brilliance. Today, celebrate what makes you feel alive. Your passion and play are magnets that attract admiration and opportunity naturally.

Affirmation & Gratitude

"I embrace joy and creativity, letting passion fuel my spirit."

Leo

26 November 2026

The Moon highlights health, routines, and productivity. You may feel motivated to organize your schedule, refine habits, or tend to lingering tasks. Wellness is key today—focus on balance through rest, movement, and nourishment. Though routines may seem mundane, they sustain your fiery ambition. Leo, discipline isn't restriction—it's empowerment. By caring for your body and daily rhythm, you fuel the brilliance that makes your roar echo strongly into the world.

Affirmation & Gratitude

"I strengthen my body and routines, creating balance that sustains my fire."

Leo

27 November 2026

The Moon moves into your partnership zone, spotlighting love, cooperation, and teamwork. Romantic connections may deepen, while collaborations in work flow with ease. If tensions linger, use empathy and patience to resolve them. Leo, your pride can sometimes resist compromise, but harmony creates resilience. Today is about valuing balance—real strength is found in connection. Share your warmth generously and relationships will flourish with trust and loyalty.

Affirmation & Gratitude

"I honor love and cooperation, creating harmony in my relationships."

Leo
28 November 2026

The Moon enters your exploration sector, sparking curiosity and a hunger for growth. You may feel inspired to travel, study, or explore spirituality. Even small steps—like journaling or engaging with fresh perspectives—ignite wisdom. Leo, your fire thrives when it's fed with discovery. Today invites you to expand horizons and step beyond comfort zones. Say yes to growth—you'll feel renewed, inspired, and more connected to your path.

Affirmation & Gratitude

"I embrace curiosity and growth, letting new horizons expand my fire."

Leo
29 November 2026

The Moon activates your career zone, drawing attention to ambition, recognition, and responsibility. Opportunities for leadership may arise, or a project could demand completion. Step into the spotlight confidently, but pair pride with humility. Leo, your roar is magnetic, but it's reliability that earns lasting respect. Today is about proving you can lead with strength and consistency. Recognition flows naturally when actions and words align with integrity.

Affirmation & Gratitude

"I step into leadership with confidence and humility, proving my strength through action."

Leo
30 November 2026

A quieter tone emerges as the Moon enters your spiritual and inner world. You may feel drawn to solitude, rest, or meditation. Intuition is heightened—listen closely to dreams and subtle insights. Though you thrive on visibility, Leo, today is about replenishing your fire through reflection. Rest isn't retreat—it's renewal. By honoring stillness, you prepare yourself for the next bold stage of your journey.

Affirmation & Gratitude

"I honor stillness and intuition, trusting reflection restores my strength."

December 2026

Leo
01 December 2026

The Moon enters your sign, amplifying confidence, vitality, and magnetism. You'll feel ready to step forward with bold action in love, work, or creativity. Others notice your glow easily—use this influence to inspire, not overshadow. Leo, today is about celebrating your authentic self unapologetically while also sharing your warmth generously. When you shine authentically, you give others permission to shine too.

Affirmation & Gratitude
"I shine authentically, inspiring others with my light and generosity."

Leo
02 December 2026

The Moon emphasizes finances and self-worth, urging you to reflect on resources and value. You may feel called to budget, save, or renegotiate. Avoid overspending—focus on stability and gratitude. Leo, true abundance isn't just wealth—it's knowing your worth and demanding respect. Today is about making practical choices that reflect your confidence and support your dreams. Prosperity follows when you align self-respect with wise action.

Affirmation & Gratitude

"I honor my worth, making wise choices that attract abundance."

Leo
03 December 2026

The Moon highlights communication, making this a strong day for sharing ideas, writing, or connecting with others. Conversations flow easily, and your words hold influence. Networking may bring opportunities, while heartfelt talks heal relationships. Be mindful of tone—balance your natural confidence with warmth and sincerity. Leo, your roar can inspire, but your thoughtful voice builds lasting loyalty. Today is about using your voice as a bridge for understanding, growth, and opportunity.

Affirmation & Gratitude

"I use my words with clarity and kindness, creating harmony and trust."

Leo
04 December 2026

The Moon shifts into your home and family zone, pulling your focus inward. Domestic responsibilities, family conversations, or simply creating peace in your living space feel important. Though your pride craves recognition outside, your roots sustain your fire. Leo, success is hollow without a strong foundation. Today is about nurturing the spaces and relationships that give you strength. Honor your roots, and you'll feel more grounded for the ambitions ahead.

Affirmation & Gratitude

"I nurture my home and family, honoring the roots that sustain me."

Leo
05 December 2026

The Moon enters your creativity and romance sector, amplifying joy, playfulness, and passion. You may feel inspired to pursue hobbies, artistic projects, or simply leisure that excites your spirit. Romance feels especially lively, and your charisma is magnetic. Professionally, creative solutions may emerge unexpectedly—follow them. Leo, joy is your superpower—it restores energy and inspires others. Today is about celebrating life with openness, letting play and passion fuel your brilliance.

Affirmation & Gratitude

"I embrace joy and creativity, letting passion guide my fire."

Leo
06 December 2026

The Moon emphasizes health, routines, and productivity. You'll feel motivated to tackle tasks, organize, or refine habits that support long-term balance. Focus on sustainable changes in wellness—movement, nutrition, and rest. Leo, discipline is not a cage—it's the structure that sustains your flame. Today is about honoring the details that keep your body and spirit strong. By investing in small acts of consistency, you empower your bigger ambitions.

Affirmation & Gratitude

"I strengthen my routines with balance and discipline, sustaining my fire."

Leo
07 December 2026

Relationships take the spotlight as the Moon activates your partnership sector. Romantic connections may deepen, or professional collaborations may move forward smoothly. If tension lingers, today brings opportunity for resolution. Cooperation and empathy are key. Leo, your pride may resist compromise, but real power is found in unity. By honoring others as much as yourself, you create bonds that grow stronger and more supportive over time.

Affirmation & Gratitude

"I honor love and cooperation, creating balance and harmony in my relationships."

Leo
03 December 2026

The Moon enters your exploration zone, stirring curiosity and adventure. You may feel inspired to travel, begin studies, or dive into new perspectives. Spiritually, breakthroughs are likely if you remain open. Even small steps—journaling, learning, or connecting with diverse people—expand your worldview. Leo, your fire thrives on discovery. Today is about stretching beyond the familiar to gain wisdom and renewal. Trust curiosity—it will guide your spirit to growth.

Affirmation & Gratitude
"I embrace curiosity and growth, letting new horizons expand my spirit."

Leo
09 December 2026

The Moon moves into your career and ambition sector, spotlighting visibility and recognition. You may feel called to step into leadership or showcase talents. Recognition is possible today if charisma is paired with reliability. Leo, your roar is magnetic, but it's your dedication that secures long-term respect. Today is about proving you can lead with both confidence and consistency. Take a bold step toward building your legacy.

Affirmation & Gratitude

"I step confidently into leadership, proving my strength through action."

Leo
10 December 2026

The Moon shifts into your spiritual and inner world, encouraging rest, reflection, and renewal. Intuition is heightened—dreams and synchronicities may carry guidance. You may crave solitude or time away from external pressures. Though your pride thrives in the spotlight, Leo, wisdom comes when you honor silence. Today is not for bold moves but for preparing your inner fire. Stillness fuels clarity, helping you make stronger choices in the days ahead.

Affirmation & Gratitude

"I honor stillness and intuition, trusting reflection strengthens my fire."

Leo
11 December 2026

The Moon enters your sign, boosting charisma, confidence, and vitality. You'll feel more visible and ready to take bold steps in love, creativity, or career. Others are drawn to your magnetism—use this influence to inspire, not dominate. Leo, today is about shining authentically, celebrating your uniqueness, and uplifting those around you with generosity. Your roar is heard, but your warmth ensures it is remembered with admiration.

Affirmation & Gratitude

"I shine authentically, inspiring others with my light and generosity."

Leo
12 December 2026

The Moon emphasizes finances and self-worth, prompting you to review resources and values. You may feel motivated to budget, save, or demand recognition for your work. Avoid impulsive spending; focus instead on choices that create long-term security. Leo, abundance grows when you align with gratitude and wisdom. Today is about affirming your value through practical steps that honor your worth and attract prosperity naturally.

Affirmation & Gratitude

"I honor my worth and make wise choices that attract abundance."

Leo
13 December 2026

The Moon highlights communication, favoring important conversations, writing, and networking. Your words carry influence today, and people are more receptive to your ideas. Professionally, presentations thrive; personally, heartfelt talks bring healing. Leo, your roar may command attention, but it's your sincerity that builds loyalty. Balance speaking with listening to create deeper understanding. Today is about using language as a tool for connection and progress.

Affirmation & Gratitude
"I use my words with clarity and kindness, creating harmony and opportunity."

Leo
14 December 2026

The Moon enters your home and family sector, urging you to ground yourself. Domestic responsibilities, family conversations, or simply enjoying comfort at home feel important. Though ambition calls, nurturing your private life sustains your outer fire. Leo, your true power grows from stability. Today is about creating peace within your sanctuary, strengthening the roots that help you shine more brightly in the wider world.

Affirmation & Gratitude

"I nurture my home and loved ones, honoring the roots that sustain me."

Leo
15 December 2026

The Moon activates your creativity and romance zone, sparking joy, play, and inspiration. You may feel drawn to hobbies, art, or romantic gestures. Passion flows more easily, and your charisma is magnetic. Professionally, innovative ideas may emerge—follow them. Leo, joy is essential, not indulgent. Today is about celebrating what makes you feel alive and sharing that spark with others. Your light attracts admiration and opportunity naturally.

Affirmation & Gratitude

"I embrace joy and creativity, letting passion fuel my spirit."

Leo
16 December 2026

The Moon emphasizes health, routines, and organization, urging you to refine habits and boost productivity. You may feel compelled to exercise, declutter, or create order. Though mundane, these efforts support your long-term fire. Leo, discipline is your ally—it sustains your brilliance and energy. Today is about making small, consistent choices that honor your body and mind, ensuring your roar echoes with strength for years to come.

Affirmation & Gratitude

"I strengthen my routines with balance and discipline, sustaining my vitality."

Leo
17 December 2026

The Moon highlights partnerships, placing relationships at the center of your day. Romantic bonds may deepen, or professional collaborations can move forward smoothly. If tension lingers, empathy and compromise will bring resolution. Leo, your pride sometimes resists giving ground, but true strength lies in connection. Today is about valuing cooperation as much as independence. When you share your warmth generously, love and loyalty return to you tenfold.

Affirmation & Gratitude
"I honor love and cooperation, creating harmony and balance in my relationships."

Leo
18 December 2026

The Moon moves into your exploration and growth zone, sparking curiosity and adventure. You may feel inspired to learn, travel, or pursue spiritual discovery. Even small actions—reading, journaling, or speaking with someone from a different perspective—expand your horizons. Leo, your fire thrives on fresh inspiration. Today is about saying yes to discovery, embracing change, and trusting that growth lies just beyond your comfort zone.

Affirmation & Gratitude
"I embrace curiosity and growth, letting new horizons expand my spirit."

Leo
19 December 2026

The Moon activates your career and recognition sector, putting you in the spotlight. Leadership opportunities may arise, or you may receive acknowledgment for your recent efforts. Step forward confidently, but let humility anchor you. Leo, your roar is magnetic, but it's your consistency that builds respect. Today is about proving that your fire is steady as well as brilliant. Recognition flows when your passion is backed with dedication.

Affirmation & Gratitude

"I step into leadership with confidence and humility, proving my strength through action."

Leo
20 December 2026

The Moon draws your focus inward as it enters your spiritual sector. You may crave solitude, rest, or meditation. Intuition is heightened—pay attention to dreams and inner whispers. Though you shine in the spotlight, Leo, wisdom is born in silence. Today is about renewal through stillness. Rest is not retreat—it's preparation for your next powerful stride. Allow yourself to recharge; it strengthens the fire within.

Affirmation & Gratitude

"I honor stillness and intuition, trusting reflection renews my fire."

Leo
21 December 2026

The Moon moves into your sign, boosting vitality, confidence, and magnetism. You'll feel eager to pursue personal goals, romance, or creativity. Others notice your presence easily—use this spotlight to inspire, not dominate. Leo, your authentic light shines brightest when it uplifts others. Today is about celebrating yourself unapologetically while reminding those around you that their brilliance matters too. Lead by example with warmth and generosity.

Affirmation & Gratitude
"I shine authentically, inspiring others with my light and warmth."

Leo

22 December 2026

The Moon emphasizes finances and self-worth, urging you to reflect on money and personal value. You may feel motivated to budget, save, or renegotiate for fairness. Avoid impulsive spending—focus on security and gratitude. Leo, true abundance flows when you respect yourself enough to make wise choices. Today is about aligning your confidence with practical actions that build long-term prosperity and stability.

Affirmation & Gratitude

"I honor my worth, making wise choices that attract abundance."

Leo

23 December 2026

The Moon highlights communication, making today excellent for conversations, networking, or creative expression. Your words carry charm and influence, so use them to connect meaningfully. Professionally, proposals or presentations thrive; personally, heartfelt talks heal or inspire. Leo, your roar commands attention, but your thoughtful words build bridges. Today is about balancing strength with compassion in speech. Communication is your key to progress and connection.

Affirmation & Gratitude

"I use my words with clarity and kindness, creating harmony and opportunity."

Leo
24 December 2026

The Moon moves into your home and family sector, reminding you to ground yourself before the year ends. You may feel drawn to nurture loved ones, decorate, or simply create comfort in your space. Emotional conversations can heal old wounds, strengthening bonds. Leo, your pride thrives in the outside world, but your roots sustain your fire. Today is about cherishing your foundation so that you step into the new year with peace and strength.

Affirmation & Gratitude

"I nurture my home and family, honoring the roots that sustain me."

Leo
25 December 2026

The Moon energizes your creativity and romance zone, filling the day with joy, play, and connection. Celebrations feel lively, and you're likely to attract admiration and affection. Hobbies, laughter, and shared activities restore your spark. Professionally, creative breakthroughs may emerge when you allow yourself to relax and have fun. Leo, joy is never wasted—it's the flame that keeps your heart alive. Today is about celebrating life unapologetically.

Affirmation & Gratitude

"I embrace joy and creativity, letting passion fuel my fire."

Leo
26 December 2026

The Moon highlights health, routines, and productivity, encouraging balance after indulgence. You may feel motivated to exercise, tidy, or restore order. Wellness choices matter more today, bringing clarity and energy. Leo, consistency fuels freedom—when you respect your body and routines, your ambitions thrive. Today is about treating discipline as self-love. Small adjustments today lay the foundation for vitality and success in the new year.

Affirmation & Gratitude

"I strengthen myself with balance and discipline, sustaining my vitality."

Leo
27 December 2026

The Moon enters your partnership zone, spotlighting love, cooperation, and teamwork. Romantic connections may feel affectionate and warm, while professional collaborations thrive. Compromise is key—avoid letting pride block harmony. Leo, your roar is powerful, but true strength lies in balance. Today is about sharing light generously and recognizing that unity brings more joy than standing alone. Relationships flourish when nurtured with empathy and respect.

Affirmation & Gratitude
"I honor love and cooperation, creating harmony in my relationships."

Leo
28 December 2026

The Moon moves into your exploration and learning zone, inspiring curiosity and fresh ideas. You may feel drawn to travel, new studies, or spiritual practices. Even small steps—reading, journaling, or engaging with different perspectives—ignite growth. Leo, your fire expands when you embrace discovery. Today is about opening your mind to wisdom and trusting that curiosity leads to freedom and inspiration.

Affirmation & Gratitude
"I embrace curiosity and growth, letting new horizons expand my spirit."

Leo
29 December 2026

The Moon activates your career sector, drawing attention to ambition and recognition. A project may come to completion, or leadership opportunities may arise. You're in the spotlight, Leo—show that your roar is backed by reliability. Recognition flows when charisma is paired with effort. Today is about aligning action with vision to strengthen your legacy. Your dedication now sets the stage for opportunities in the coming year.

Affirmation & Gratitude

"I step into leadership with confidence and humility, proving my strength through action."

Leo

30 December 2026

The Moon shifts into your spiritual and inner world, encouraging reflection as the year closes. You may crave solitude, meditation, or quiet rituals to honor your journey. Intuition is strong—listen closely to dreams and subtle messages. Leo, this is not about endings but renewal. By pausing now, you prepare for a vibrant new chapter. Today is about gratitude, release, and inner peace as you step into 2027.

Affirmation & Gratitude

"I honor reflection and release, trusting renewal awaits in the new year."

Leo
31 December 2026

The Moon remains in your spiritual sector, guiding you to slow down and reflect as the year closes. This is a powerful day for gratitude rituals, journaling, or meditation. Release what no longer serves you and honor the lessons learned. Leo, your roar has echoed loudly in 2026, but today is about gentle closure. By embracing reflection, you prepare yourself for renewal. Spend time with loved ones, but carve out quiet moments to connect with your inner flame. Peace is your gift today.

Affirmation & Gratitude

"I release the old with gratitude, welcoming renewal as the year tur

www.ingramcontent.com/pod-product-compliance
Lightning Source LLC
Chambersburg PA
CBHW071145070526
44584CB00019B/2670